HAUNTED HOOS
INDIANA UNIVERSITY

Kat Klockow

4880 Lower Valley Road, Atglen, Pennsylvania 19310

Other Schiffer Books on Related Subjects:

Creepy Colleges and Haunted Universities: True Ghost Stories, 0-7643-1805-5, $9.95

Indiana Ghost Folklore, 978-0-7643-3334-7, $14.99

Strange Indiana Monsters, 0-7643-2608-2, $12.95

Schiffer Books are available at special discounts for bulk purchases for sales promotions or premiums. Special editions, including personalized covers, corporate imprints, and excerpts can be created in large quantities for special needs. For more information contact the publisher:

Published by Schiffer Publishing Ltd.
4880 Lower Valley Road
Atglen, PA 19310
Phone: (610) 593-1777; Fax: (610) 593-2002
E-mail: Info@schifferbooks.com

For the largest selection of fine reference books on this and related subjects, please visit our web site at: **www.schifferbooks.com**

We are always looking for people to write books on new and related subjects. If you have an idea for a book please contact us at the above address.

This book may be purchased from the publisher. Include $5.00 for shipping. Please try your bookstore first. You may write for a free catalog.

In Europe, Schiffer books are distributed by:
Bushwood Books
6 Marksbury Ave.
Kew Gardens
Surrey TW9 4JF England
Phone: 44 (0) 20 8392 8585; Fax: 44 (0) 20 8392 9876
E-mail: info@bushwoodbooks.co.uk
Website: www.bushwoodbooks.co.uk

Designed by Stephanie Daugherty
Type set in Eraser/NewBskvll BT/Gill Sans MT

ISBN: 978-0-7643-3574-7
Printed in the United States of America

ACKNOWLEDGMENTS

O h, the acknowledgments section... The special section of a book where the author thanks those who have helped them and the book become what it is today. A place of honor and reverence, it's usually is skipped over by eager readers and only read after they have finished the book. In all seriousness, though, there are a few people who I really owe a debt of gratitude to for one reason or another. There are exactly seven people who have helped make this book possible; some who are into the paranormal and some who aren't: Mike, Dave and Liz, Marlene and Ericka, and Lisa and Melanie.

 Mike is my husband and my delightful skeptic. I can show him photos of "ghosts" or have him listen to EVPs and he'll bring a rational approach to figuring out what they are. He keeps me from sailing off into the clouds from time to time, and I really appreciated his help while writing this book. Thanks for hanging in there, love!

 Dave and Liz are my parents, and you'll probably notice that many of the illustrations of the campus are done by Liz Fuller, my dear old mom. An artist, she taught me since I was a wee one how to illustrate, though I don't think she thought I would grow up to become a comic book illustrator and paranormal author. Dave, my dad, is a wonderful man who always made sure I was safe and sound. Because of his sacrifices, I was able to do so many things. I thank you both for letting me look into the paranormal.

 Marlene and Ericka have contributed more to my personality than even they know. Marlene is an old family friend who bought me my first ghost book, *Haunted Ohio* by Chris Woodyard, back in 1993. Ericka has been my best friend since high school, and we have gone on many paranormal explorations around South Bend, Indiana, together. She's always helping me to look at the world in different perspectives and cheering me on in my endeavors.

 Finally, I want to thank Lisa and Melanie; these two members of Indiana Ghost Trackers are mentioned numerous times in this book. I met them when I first walked into the Indiana Ghost Trackers meeting in January 2009, and being Bloomington locals, they were able to help me look into many local haunts — and have gone beyond merely helping me compile a book about ghosts and goblins around their town. These two women have become great friends of mine. Thanks guys, and here's to many more happy hunts to come!

Oh, who am I we kidding? I can't discount the awesome investigators from the Bloomington/South Central chapter of Indiana Ghost Trackers for their help and support. Thank you Angie, Cloud — oops I mean Claude, Traci, Kevin, Maria, Dean, and last but not least, Rob.

There is also one more person I would like to thank. I have never personally met him since he died eleven years before I was born, but he's the inspiration for all of my paranormal investigations. My Grandpa Eddy... If I hadn't seen your blue-silhouetted form walk up that old flight of stairs one night in 1992, I wouldn't be who I am today.

CONTENTS

INTRODUCTION

Welcome to the haunted halls of Indiana University Bloomington and the ghostly back roads of Southern Indiana! This is a book I have wanted to write for a while now, and thankfully I have been given the chance to bring some of Southern Indiana's ghost stories to light. Some of these stories have been shared via oral narrative and haven't been recorded before in a book while other locations haven't been included in books of this nature before, such as Whispers Estate.

Indiana University (simply known as IU) is one of the largest and oldest universities in the state. IU is one of two Big Ten Conference Universities in the state of Indiana; the other being long-standing rival Purdue University, the home of the Boilermakers. Of course, with any campus as old as Indiana University, there are ghost stories all around the campus. Some of them are variations of other well-known urban legends, such as the Hatchet Man of McNutt Quadrangle. Other stories are purely Indiana University's, such as our ghostly Girl in Yellow who resides in Read Hall, or the strange Lady in Black that has been seen wandering Third Street since 1911.

IU, however, isn't the only haunted place in Southern Indiana. Oh, no. The City of Bloomington also has many stories of the paranormal to offer: there is the infamous Portico's

One of many gargoyles that sit atop Maxwell Hall on Indiana University Bloomington's campus. *Illustration by Liz Fuller.*

Restaurant and its ghostly children who startled patrons for twelve years, Rose Hill Cemetery and its creepy shadow people, and a cluster of schools that really have "spirit." Looking beyond the city limits of Bloomington are more stories of the strange and supernatural: Whispers Estate and its ghostly hostess Rachel, the spectral children at Tunnelton Tunnel, and the phantom actors of Crump Theater.

While collecting stories and photos for this book, I tried to personally visit as many locations as possible. My background is in Cultural Anthropology, and thus I treat each haunted location as fieldwork. Those who have investigated with me will agree that I go around locations with a watch, clipboard, and audio recorder in hand...along with every ghost hunter's buddy — the flashlight. During investigations, I am making note of every person present, what tools investigators are using, and any noises and odd phenomena that occur, as well as sketching the location. When I look into the paranormal, I am constantly looking for how the living and the dead relate to one another. How are the supposed spirits of the dead communicating with the living? Are the folktales and legends of the supernatural based in fact or fiction? Does local history support these ghost stories? The questions are never-ending.

There are really too many ghost stories from Southern Indiana to put down to writing in one book. Whether you are a visitor, student, or resident of Bloomington or Indiana University, this book is here for you to get to know the ghostly history of the town and campus and the countryside that surrounds the two. Please enjoy it, and I hope you can get some sleep tonight!

NOTES FROM THE AUTHOR

Riddled throughout this book are jargon, phrases, and abbreviations commonly used in the paranormal investigative field. This book's main focus is ghost stories, so related terminology is used to explain some of the haunts around Indiana. Since I don't assume every reader of this book is familiar with terms used in the paranormal field, I will explain what they mean here. Abbreviations are handy because they shorten ridiculously long terms into very short, practical, and manageable bits of vernacular. So let's begin.

EVPs

The most common abbreviation in this book is "EVP," which stands for Electronic Voice Phenomena. An EVP is a recorded audible noise that wasn't originally heard by investigators during the investigation.

EVPs can be voices, screams, growls, moans...you name it. They don't have to be human; ghosts of animals and entities not assumed to have ever been human have also been recorded. EVPs don't need to appear in English either; they can be recorded in any language. There is a hypothesis within the paranormal community that spirits are able to understand and communicate in any language that they choose.

Some paranormal investigative groups have classified EVPs into three classes: "A," "B," and "C," depending on how clear the recorded sound is. "Class A" EVPS are clear and easily distinguishable from the rest of the background talking and noises on the recording. "Class B" EVPs are a little more difficult to hear and are generally whispers that are mostly distinguishable. Personally, I think this is the most common type of EVP recorded. The final category is "Class C," which are indistinguishable and unintelligible sounds that seem out of place with the rest of the recording. The recording sounds like something was trying to communicate, but you just can't understand it. These types are also pretty common — and quite frustrating for paranormal investigators.

Similar to an EVP is the disembodied voice. These are the voices, moans, and whispers that can be heard in real time without the aid of recording. The Whispers Estate in Mitchell, Indiana, actually gets its name from this type of haunting. The house is known for being a *mecca* of disembodied voices. Sometimes hearing disembodied voices can be quite jarring or frightening — even to seasoned investigators — because they happen so suddenly.

Another subject to point out while on the topic of EVPs is the EVP session performed at a ghost hunt or investigation. At this point in the hunt, team members will quietly sit in the area they are investigating and ask questions to the spirits residing in that location. After each question, there is a three to five second pause to allow time for the spirit to reply. Sometimes this tactic helps with capturing evidence of the paranormal...sometimes it doesn't. While on investigations, I prefer to do both a "stiff" EVP question session (when investigators ask questions as described above) and a "relaxed" EVP session (where investigators chit-chat about whatever is on their mind at the time, usually with the location's history in mind). From the data I've collected over the years, I have discovered that more EVPs are captured while participating in a "relaxed" EVP session. Why this is I don't know, but I suspect it has something to do with the tone in which we're speaking. Perhaps it is more welcoming to the spirits than the rigid questions.

Hauntings

Ghosts are funny. From their personalities to their behavior, how they react to the living is always of interest to me. Ghosts don't always just pop out of a wall and say "howdy-do!" to the lucky individual who runs across them. Like the living, their personalities determine how they act and relate to the things around them. Most paranormal investigators will agree that there are two main categories for haunting: a residual haunting and an intelligent haunting.

A *residual haunting* can be described best as an old movie playing out to the witnesses; nothing that is happening is interactive with the world around it. Good examples of a residual haunting are Ann Boleyn in the Tower of London, England, who is seen walking the grounds on the anniversary of her death; spectral armies fighting in Gettysburg, Pennsylvania; or even the phantom suicide jumpers off the Tojinbou Cliffs in Sakai, Japan. Popular thought on these phenomena is that residual haunts are replaying past traumatic events that were literally recorded into the surrounding environment. If you ever find yourself face-to-face with Paula, the tragic Resident Assistant, falling down the stairs in Read Dormitory or the Lady in Black at Stepp Cemetery, rest assured that these are just playbacks of more emotional times...you won't be harmed.

Intelligent Hauntings are encounters with spirits that are aware of and interact with the living. It is believed by some that these spirits retain their former personalities, and thus act much in the same way they did while alive. Some interactive ghosts do not realize that they have passed away. Others, though, do — and they take pleasure in staying with living people they now find familiar. The La Casa Lady at Indiana University, the ghosts of Greyfrier's Cemetery in Edinburgh, Scotland, and the spirits at Myrtle's Plantation in St. Francisville, Louisiana, are all examples of interactive spirits roving around the world.

Collecting Evidence of a Ghost

Methods of paranormal investigating differs from group to group. So it is understandable for those who are new to the community to be confused about what is proper procedure and what isn't. In this book, I refer to two different types of data collection — the hunt and the investigation — and I try not to use the terms interchangeably since there is a difference in field experience in order to participate in one from the other.

A hunt, or ghost hunt, is an informally structured exploration of an allegedly haunted site that usually allows a larger group of people to visit. Sites can be private, but usually are public locations such as cemeteries or parks and only last for an hour or two. Ghost hunts are *not* complete investigations.

The structured version of a ghost hunt is an investigation. This is generally what is *supposed* to be depicted to viewers via television shows like "Ghost Hunters" or "Paranormal State." In an investigation, small groups of four to five people spend up to ten hours collecting visual, audio, and photographic data at the request of the location's owner. Depending on the group, members could be trying to either legitimately prove or disprove a reported haunting.

~~~~~

There you have it...some notes about the book to keep in mind while reading. I hope this section has been informative to you, the reader! You may have noticed that I refer to ghosts as factual entities; this is because I have encountered far too many unexplained events in my life to count them out completely. Although when I investigate a location, I never assume I will find any evidence of the paranormal. If you are a seasoned paranormal investigator or just starting out, I hope you find this book interesting and informative. The paranormal is something I have loved my entire life, and I am proud to bring you this collection of stories from Indiana University and Southern Indiana.

Cheers!

Kat
The Urban Legends Detective

MEET THE TEAMS

I wouldn't have been able to write this book without the help of some of Indiana's paranormal investigative teams who so kindly shared their data and personal experiences with me and I would like to introduce to you now the five featured paranormal groups in this book: Indiana Ghost Trackers, SHADOWS of Indiana, Hoosier Paranormal Research, The Phantom Tribe, and Midwestern Researchers and Investigators of Paranormal Activity. Each group approaches the unexplained and the subject of the paranormal in their own particular way, but are willing to share their experiences with those who ask.

INDIANA GHOST TRACKERS

www.indianaghosts.org

Founded in July of 2000 by Mike McDowell, Indiana Ghost Trackers (IGT) has quickly grown into a statewide organization that strives to unite the subject of paranormal investigations with the community in order to increase public awareness of the paranormal. One of the services that make IGT unique is inviting the public to monthly ghost hunts and chapter meetings. It was through this that I became a member of IGT Lafayette's chapter in August 2007. The organization also conducts private investigations with only fully trained members of the organization at the request of private home and business owners at no cost to the client and they participate in cleaning up "abandoned" graveyards and cemeteries that haven't seen attention in years.

Currently IGT has thirteen active chapters across the state of Indiana and the city of Chicago with over 450 active members. These chapters are Northwest, LaPorte, Michiana (Mishawaka, Elkhart, South Bend, and the southern Michigan region), South Lake, Rochester, Lafayette, Indianapolis, Fort Wayne, Kokomo, South Central (Bloomington, Columbus, and Seymour), Terre Haute, Chicago, and Muncie.

The organization uses the scientific method to collect data in order to understand what is occurring at a particular investigation site. Keeping an open mind, however, they also utilize mediums, psychics, and sensitives. More "mystical" forms of investigating such as dowsing rods and pendulums are used as well to add subjective data and compare it to the objective data collected. IGT largely concentrates their efforts on ghosts, but have been known to chase after some urban legends as well.

For most of this book I worked with the Bloomington chapter of IGT, headed by Lisa Bradley. Compared to some other chapters in the organization, the Bloomington chapter is fairly recent, as it was only established in 2006. Similar to some other chapters, though, they have a small group of members, but what they lack in manpower they make up for in commitment, with members making every meeting rain or shine. Currently there are about a dozen members who take part in the meetings every month, and often they are joined by other chapters' members (such as Indianapolis or Terre Haute members). One nice advantage to the IGT family is that members can visit other chapter's hunts, creating a "family" of members who are able to visit and hunt in areas of the state they normally would not be able to visit. There is even a traveling trophy awarded to the chapter who travels the most frequently to other chapter meetings. As of this date, the trophy is in Fort Wayne, but who knows where it will be in the coming months!

SHADOWS OF INDIANA

www.shadowsofindiana.com

A recent addition to the paranormal investigative scene is the Seekers Hunters and Debunkers of Wandering Spirits (SHADOWS) Indiana chapter. Founded in October 2006, SHADOWS is a group rooted in the scientific method. "We investigate with the purpose of trying to debunk everything we can, so what evidence we have left over is beyond our understanding and can be considered in the realm of the paranormal," writes Amanda Futlz, one of the group's founding members.

SHADOWS uses a variety of equipment to record and document data, such as handheld cameras, audio recorders, electromagnetic field (EMF) detectors, motion detectors, temperature gauges, and a four-camera DVR system. With this mix of technology, SHADOWS looks to 'debunk,' or refute, stories of ghosts and spirits among the Hoosier countryside.

SHADOWS of Indiana was founded after a group of friends shared their personal paranormal experiences. "We wanted to find an explanation and try to find some answers for what we had experienced," writes Amanda. "We share the same curiosity, for that is why I, and many other investigators out there, became paranormal investigators in the first place."

The team has done a lot with the Hannah House and Whispers Estate, two renowned haunted homes within the Hoosier state. Several of the members volunteer at the Hannah House and help run the monthly ghost hunts hosted there. The team is in touch with both Jarret Marshall and Van Renier, who both have lived in and owned the Whispers

Estate. They have also put in hours of time helping to restore Whispers Estate to make it into the home it is now. In addition to local places, SHADOWS has visited haunted national landmarks such as Waverly Hills Sanatorium and Talbot Tavern in Kentucky, Moundsville Prison the Trans Allegheny Lunatic Asylum in West Virginia, and Mineral Springs Hotel in Illinois.

HOOSiER PARANORMAL RESEARCH

www.hoosierparanormal.com

Heralding out of Edinburgh, Indiana, Hoosier Paranormal Research, or HPR, was established November 25, 2005, and has traveled all over the state to investigate, and possibly demystify, accounts of the strange and unexplained. HPR is a very structured group, working with clients on investigations to fully understand the nature of the situation taking place. Family history, property history, and environmental data are all collected and assessed when a client calls them to investigate their home, office, or property.

Firm believers in the paranormal, HPR uses the scientific method to rule out any natural phenomenon as the cause of any reported paranormal phenomena. This means HPR captures data in order to validate a client's haunting, but strives to filter out all other natural causes. The team may investigate a location several times before coming to a final determination. Furthermore, HPR fully discloses what unexplained phenomenon was found during an investigation to the client and offers suggestions of how the client may be able to manage it. Though not affiliated with any religious or spiritual group, HPR will, nevertheless, put clients in contact with the appropriate persons if the need arises.

THE PHANTOM TRIBE

www.thephantomtribe.com

Another Indiana paranormal investigative group active with the Whispers Estate, The Phantom Tribe has visited many haunted locations all over the state: Greenlawn Cemetery, Boone Hutcheson Cemetery, Cry Baby Bridge, Werewolf Hollow, Central State Hospital, and Stepp Cemetery. Phantom Tribe also has investigated many private homes in addition to the numerous public locations listed on their website.

The Phantom Tribe uses numerous pieces of equipment when investigating: four digital cameras ranging from professional level to point and shoot cameras, four Olympus digital voice recorders, a night vision camcorder, EMF detectors, an Infrared thermometer, parabolic microphone, dowsing rods, and the ghost hunter's buddy — flashlights.

MRIPA

(Midwestern Research & Investigators of Paranormal Activity)

www.mripa.net

With a fourteen-person team in the state and four out-of-state representatives, Midwestern Research and Investigators of Paranormal Activity (MRIPA) is a very active investigative team. Driving their famous MRIPA truck decked out in green lights, the team investigates not only haunted locations, but also UFO sightings and cryptozoological reports throughout the Midwestern states and beyond. MRIPA's founder, Jason Baker, stresses that the group is not one of "ghost hunters," but rather a team that researches the unexplained.

Established in 1996 under the name Xgen, in 2006 the team separated from its Xgen roots and formally became the Midwestern Research and Investigators of Paranormal Activity. Jason's group isn't out there running around cemeteries looking for a quick scare. Oh, no...this team is a serious group of investigators.

Like many groups around the state and country, MRIPA is a not-for-profit group, never charging a single cent for their investigative services. Utilizing their experience in professional trades and knowledge of technology, MRIPA explores the "possibilities of the unknown" at either requested investigations or visits to locations rumored to be haunted. Staying open-minded, the group works to uncover the truth rather than working using popular mythology.

MRIPA also keeps in contact with other local, state, national, and even international paranormal groups to share their knowledge and resources. The team has traveled all over the globe looking into stories of the unexplained, including Beijing, China, Munich, Germany, Blarney Castle, McHugh Park, Blackrock Castle, and Jacobs Island Ruins in Ireland, along with numerous locations in the Midwest and around the country. MRIPA has also visited two locations featured in this book: Crump Theater and Stepp Cemetery.

1

CAMPUS
GHOST STORIES
& LEGENDS

IU'S MISCELLANEOUS SPOOKS AND SPECTERS

Since Indiana University is one of the oldest universities in Indiana, it only seems reasonable that there would be a few ghosts that have cropped up around the property. These groups of ghosts are more elusive than their peers, so stories about them are rare, but exist nonetheless.

The Phantoms of the Arboretum

Located off of 10th Street, across from the Kelley School of Business and next to the Herman B. Wells Main Library, sits the extensive green space known as the Arboretum. During the day, the Arboretum is a pleasant place to take a stroll, especially in the springtime. However, at night, the atmosphere within the Arboretum turns a bit creepier.

The plot of land that the Arboretum now occupies was once the location of the 10th Street Stadium; built in 1925, the stadium could hold (at that time) an impressive 20,000 people within its stands. The stadium became famous for being the setting of the 1979 film "Breaking Away," a movie about the Little 500 bicycle race that takes place annually on campus. In 1979, however, the 10th Street Stadium was razed and the location made into the Arboretum; since then sporting events have taken place in and around the Memorial Stadium area.

Reported paranormal activity coming from the Arboretum includes a raspy voice yelling "get off my home!" Other people have claimed seeing a dark, shadowy looking apparition darting along the Arboretum's edge, trailing them until they have left the area. A shadow figure of a man has also been seen standing near the weeping willow in the center of the arboretum next to the pond. A campus legend mentions that one student drowned in the pond in the 1980s, however nothing has been found to back the story up from a factual point of view.

Whatever it is that haunts the arboretum, it does not like guests. At night, the quicker you can walk through the area, the better!

Wright Quadrangle's Lady in Black

Located where North Jordan Avenue and 10th Street intersect, Wright Quadrangle is known for being the center of campus life. Its convenient location to the rest of the campus makes Wright an attractive area to live for freshmen and sophomore students. Originally titled the Men's

Quadrangle, it was renamed in 1959 after former Indiana Governor Joseph A. Wright (1849-1857). In the Little 500, Wright Quadrangle is the home of two well-known cycling teams: the all-male Dodd's House and all-female Wright Cycledelics.

The organization of the dormitory makes it prime for ghosts to lurk. The residence hall is divided up into eighteen "houses" that are connected by hallways, breezeways, and stairwells — and that creates many dark corners ripe for eerie activity. Among those hiding in the "shadows" is a phantom dubbed the "Lady in Black." Not related to the dark apparition often reported to glide along East Third Street, this shadowy figure is far more elusive. She is most often seen around the laundry rooms of Wright Quadrangle, but darts away from view when noticed. Is she a true ghost or a trick of light? Dorm residents aren't quite sure.

The Phantom Swimmer

One of the most bizarre and infrequently told stories is that of the Student Building Swimmer, a ghost that supposedly haunts the wood floor hallways around the Anthropology and Geography departments. According to the legend, in the early years of the Student Building there used to be a pool. One day, many years ago, a male undergraduate dove into the shallow end of the pool breaking his neck, killing him instantly. Now the ghost of the student is said to have been seen swimming along the floor of the student building, only his bobbing head and upper arms visible.

However, this story doesn't hold much water. The Student Building, the only campus building with a bell tower, was built in 1906 specifically to house the Anthropology and Geography departments, classrooms, and labs. Alumni and students raised the funds to erect the building, which is why it's called the Student Building. In 1970, the Indiana University museum was moved into the building from Maxwell Hall. The building saw a facelift in 1991, as the entire structure was renovated for the approaching twenty-first century. Like many of the Old Crescent buildings on campus, the Student Building has been added to the National Register of Historic Places. No pool has ever existed in the Student Building.

The Lilly's Invisible Visitors

During my time at Indiana University, there were few buildings that I never stepped a foot into — the Lilly Library was, unfortunately, one of them. I regret this now. While doing research for this book, I found out that the building and its exhibits seem like some of the best treasures located on campus. The Lilly Library, which is part of the Indiana University Library System, is special; within its sandstone walls lay exhibits of the special collections. Plus, rare books and manuscripts can be read here. It is one of the few places in the world where you can look at an authentic copy the *Tibetan Book of the Dead* and read the original "Batman" comic books...all while listening to live performances by local musicians.

The Lilly Library sits in the Fine Arts Plaza next to the IU Auditorium, across from Showalter Fountain. It was dedicated October 3, 1960 as a place to house the countless rare books and manuscripts that J.K. Lilly Jr. donated to Indiana University Bloomington in 1956 and 1957. These articles are still on display at the library for the public to see daily along with traveling exhibits visiting the University.

To make the Lilly Library even more interesting is the ghost stories that surround its exhibits. Because of the nature of the materials it houses, many students, visitors, and staff members have reported seeing or hearing things around the building that are unexplained. A hypothesis within the paranormal community is that ghosts can become attached to items they enjoyed in life. Perhaps this is the case here since staff members have reported hearing ghostly conversations when they are alone in the building as well as footsteps following behind them. Other reported phenomena are ghostly shadows moving along the corridors in the building and small items being moved around by unseen hands. Visitors have felt a heavy atmosphere at exhibitions only to have it disappear after the exhibit moves on to a new location. Though the stories are chilling, to date none of Lilly Library's invisible guests has harmed anyone.

Reflections

Indiana University is a diverse and historically rich campus. As more and more students come into the campus culture, they help shape and continue the oral narratives they have heard from previous university students. Some students have heard the stories from their older siblings and bring them back to the campus to share with their new friends, while others simply hear the legends from older students residing on campus. Transferring stories from one generation to another is a way of preserving history, and nowhere is that better illustrated than in the form of ghost stories.

While their mythos has been hyped up over time, some of these ghost stories may have very earthly explanations. The phantom in the Arboretum is a fine example of this — it could have been created from a tired student's imagination running wild at night. It is completely plausible that due to poor lighting and distance between passersby in the Arboretum that students walking through quietly at night were "mis-identified" as ghosts. Becoming uneasy and panicking in secluded locations is natural... and sometimes ghost stories are the end result.

THE LADY IN BLACK

One of the oldest and best known ghost stories from IU's Bloomington campus is the "Lady in Black" of East Third Street. Her tale has sent shivers down the spines of generations of Indiana University students and alumni — and sent a few screaming down the street on occasion.

Her Mysterious Legend

Not much is known about her background, but since 1911 there have been reported sightings of her dark silhouette floating along the paths in the old parts of campus. The Lady in Black has been said to haunt the Old Crescent section of campus, but her favorite haunt is on Third Street around the fraternity and sorority houses that line the road.

According to the reports, the Lady in Black wears a long, black, bustled dress in the fashion of the late Victorian Era, which sets her noticeably apart from other pedestrians on the street. Reports also have her wearing a black lace veil with a hat that covers her face while carrying a large, open umbrella or lace parasol that she twirls as she glides silently along the sidewalks at a walking pace, sometimes following young couples walking the streets late at night or early in the morning. Most witnesses say she is nearly a full-bodied, non-transparent apparition...except that her dress fades away where her feet would be located. She also can appear as a shadowy entity around the streets.

The Lady in Black has also been seen chasing lonely fraternity members down Third Street late at night, especially around Halloween. This report gave rise to the idea that possibly she was actually a man in disguise, since she was running much faster than any average woman could run. Sightings of her have persisted randomly through the decades. The ghost has also been seen at a Women's League Halloween Party, announcing that she would return to campus every Halloween night to haunt the street, which is probably her most well known appearance.

Through the years she has been reported by passersby along the streets from the hours of midnight to 3 o'clock in the morning, commonly known as the "witching hours." Sometimes police officers patrolling the neighborhood have mistaken her as a burglar, but when approached for questioning, she disappears in front of their eyes.

The Lady in Black has been witnessed silently floating down Third Street since 1911.
Illustration by Kat Klockow.

Mystery Solved?

In 1921, the *Indiana Daily Student* ran a story about how a mentally unstable woman was found to be stalking students around the campus. When she was caught, she was wearing all black clothing and it was concluded that she was in fact the mysterious "Lady in Black." That speculation quickly crumbled, however, when more sightings of the ghostly woman were reported later that year by students and residents of the neighborhood around Third Street. The catch was that the mentally unstable woman was still in the custody of the Bloomington Police Department.

Some have speculated by her description that the Lady in Black is a widow mourning her husband or other family member since the dress she is often described wearing is similar to a Victorian "mourning outfit." Perhaps she was a professor's widow at the turn-of-the-twentieth century. Her true identity remains as mysterious as her appearances, fleeting glimpses into Bloomington's past. Through the years, she has become a beloved mascot of Halloween for some groups, with students looking for her every October 31st, and her story is retold at the annual Folklore Office's Ghost Walk.

Reflections

A true Indiana University classic tale of the paranormal, the Lady in Black's haunting legacy is retold every year to a new batch of wide-eyed freshmen around campus. Her tale is as much beloved by campus ghost enthusiasts as the ghosts of Read Hall and the Career Development Center. Her legend will continue to live on *far, far* into the future.

THE EIGHTH STREET GHOST

If you were to walk down East Eighth Street, eventually you would come to the intersection of North Fess Avenue. There, you would see a non-descript open lot among the old homes sitting along the streets in the shadow of the Indiana Memorial Union. This lot currently plays host to a hearty vegetable garden, which is tended to by the neighborhood, but more than twenty years ago, this bare lot was home to the Zeta Beta Tau fraternity house.

The Background

The university owns much of the neighborhood property surrounding the northwest side of the campus, with many of the previous residential homes now used as department offices, such as the Department of Folklore and Ethnomusicology, the Latino Culture Center (aka La Casa), and the Asian Culture Center. At one time, fraternities and sororities rented homes to use as their organization's house before fraternity row on North Jordan Avenue was popularized. One such group was the Zeta Beta Tau Fraternity.

Zeta Beta Tau (nicknamed the "Zebes" on many campuses) were historically a predominantly Jewish fraternity, although at present they now are a nonsectarian and international fraternity with more than 130,000 members and eighty chapter locations across the globe. Indiana University is home to the Beta Gamma chapter of Zeta Beta Tau.

The Haunting Case

On the evening of October 20, 1984, Zeta Beta Tau hosted a party at their residence and, during the course of the evening, a couple of fights broke out between fraternity members and one particular guest, Jerry Zook, a former IU student who had ceased taking classes and was at the time residing in Indianapolis.

Zook, who held a grudge against one or more members of Zeta Beta Tau, snuck back into the fraternity house in the wee hours of October 21st and set the house ablaze. The fire, one of only a handful of fires to ever have taken place on the campus, injured thirty people. This may have been only what Zook meant to do, however one poor soul perished in the blaze — a nineteen-year-old former student named Israel Edelman who had been visiting the chapter that weekend. Edelman had been sleeping on the second floor of the house when the fire broke out, and he died due to smoke inhalation in his sleep.

Soon after the tragedy, Zook was arrested. The house had been gutted by the blaze, and the fraternity decided to move to a new house on North Jordan Avenue instead of rebuilding on the burnt site. There is a memorial to Edelman's memory that stands in the front of the new fraternity house.

However, since the fatal blaze, stories about a ghost seen on Eighth Street have permeated the student body. According to the rumors, passersby have detected the smell of smoke while others have heard strange disembodied voices originating from the abandoned plot of land. There are even stories of the sighting of a dark shadow person roaming along the plot, which has scared random late-night walkers around the area. For a few years, students avoided walking in that area for fear of running into the ghost.

Reflections

Is this the ghost of Israel Edelman? It isn't completely clear, however the ghost was only reported to have been seen in the years directly following the tragic blaze. In this case, the living had actively avoided the area of the fire in fear of meeting the spirit of a deceased peer. As time has continued on, though, Edelman's public memory has faded as well as the frequency of the reports of the Eighth Street Ghost. In this case, I believe that the ghost was likely a figment of morbid popular imagination, which is a common social phenomenon to occur after a horrific ordeal. Nowadays, if you asked a current IU student about the ghost or the accident, most will be completely unaware that such an event ever took place.

FEAR ON THE 11ᵀᴴ FLOOR

Indiana University has many impressive buildings on campus; one of these is the Herman B. Wells Main Library. Located on the corner of Jordan Avenue and 10ᵗʰ Street in the center of the campus, the building features double towers of Indiana limestone with a modern look. A mammoth of a building, the main library has been serving the academic and social needs of IU students since 1969, with an astounding 4.6 million volumes of books in addition to periodicals, film, and other media. It is also a central location for students to gather in its popular main lobby, spacious computer labs, special study rooms, and cyber café. The Herman B. Wells Main Library is the flagship library of the Indiana University library system that spans twenty libraries across the campus.

Scholarly History

Built in 1969, the building was just termed the "main library"; this all changed on June 17, 2005, when the library was renamed the Herman B. Wells Main Library in honor of the former Indiana University chancellor and president who had passed away five years earlier. Back in 1969, when Herman B. Wells dedicated the building, he famously said, "There is not distinguished a university without a great library." It is this library, along with the post World War II construction and reorganization of college academics, that has made IU such a strong research university in the United States.

The Stories

For all the grandeur that the library has brought to the university, however, it does have a mysterious side. The eleventh floor of the undergraduate stacks is said to harbor an entity that spreads a "creepy" impression. There are a few factors that contribute to this. First, the eleventh floor is not accessible via the elevator; it can only be accessed by taking the elevator to the tenth floor and then taking the emergency stairwell up to the eleventh. Second, unlike the other floors in the library, there isn't a university department collection assigned to that floor, so very few students have reason to venture up there. Those brave students who have explored the eleventh floor have felt as if something was watching them from behind the bookshelves. The eerie silence of the eleventh floor only adds to the uneasy environment.

The Herman B. Wells Main Library as seen from the Arboretum... *Illustration by Liz Fuller.*

There is also another rumor that has circulated around campus for a number of years, telling that some students have been a bit naughty in the "abandoned" stacks of the main library. Perhaps the ghost stories told about the eleventh floor are really only trying to cover up the acts of some students, acting more as a deterrent to keep normally studious students from interrupting anything going on up there.

Reflections

As a student on campus I had heard both rumors about the main library — and neither story I thought was too credible. To my knowledge, no deaths have occurred on the premises of the library. However it is quite possible that a former student or professor could have been very attached to the library, even in death, and haunts the place they loved so dearly. It should be noted that no apparitions, mists, whispers, or other paranormal experiences have ever been reported on the eleventh floor...just the "eerie feelings." The uneasy feelings could be explained by the poor electrical shielding of lights or wiring up on the top floor. If this is the case, then nothing paranormal is actually occurring on the top floor of the undergraduate tower.

POOR MICHAEL

Not all of the ghost stories on campus stem from suicides or victims of serial killers; some are those from horrible accidents. In the case of Poor Michael, he is a dutiful ghost fulfilling tasks he was given just before his death back in the 1960s.

Lingering Legend

In 1908, Indiana held a homecoming carnival, an event during "Gala Week," for the opening of three new university buildings. Since then the festivities have evolved into a huge celebration for the first home football game of the season. It was during such a week in the mid-1960s when our story takes place. The theme for that year's homecoming parade was "Gun Down the Hawks of Iowa," since the first intercollegiate team that the Indiana Hoosiers were playing against that year was the University of Iowa Hawks.

The parade was traveling steadily down the main streets of campus, and on one float sat an old cannon that discharged confetti and streamers every so often to the cheers of the spectators. Members of the Sigma Phi Epsilon Fraternity were present that day watching the parade go by their fraternity house. One particular member was a pledge by the name of Michael Pfang who was sitting on the curb with his buddies enjoying the celebration. As the cannon float approached the fraternity's house, it lit to sound off another wave of excitement for the football game. Unfortunately, as the float with the cannon passed by Michael, it backfired, sending shrapnel flying through the air. The largest piece sliced Michael through the neck, blowing his head off his shoulders.

Fraternity Spirit

According to members of the Sigma Phi Epsilon Fraternity, Poor Michael seems to have taken up residence in their old house since his death. It is believed that whenever anything odd occurred in the house, Michael was the perpetrator. Objects getting thrown around the house or falling off of shelves and sounds of footsteps…fraternity members living in the house had even seen Michael's apparition.

A past member claimed that Michael visited him one night while he was sleeping in his room. According to the member, who remains anonymous, he woke up in the middle of the night to find Michael standing at the door to his room. He knew it was Michael because the apparition fit the description of this former fraternity member that he had heard about from older fraternity brothers. Later, when the member questioned his fraternity brothers about the apparition, they replied that they had seen him in the house as well.

One portion of the house in particular seems to be a hotspot for the odd phenomenon — the basement. According to legend, Michael's last duties while living were to clean the basement's bathroom toilets every evening before heading for bed. Late at night fraternity members have heard the sound of moving buckets, running water with the distinct sound of scrubbing, and whistling coming from the bathroom. Even if a fraternity brother does not believe in ghosts, they are still quick to accuse Michael of being behind any odd experiences they encounter or missing objects in the house.

Reflections

Sigma Phi Epsilon has since moved out of the building, and the house now stands vacant. However, they aren't the only fraternity associated with this campus legend. The Kappa Sigma Fraternity has also been linked with the story of Poor Michael's ghost. In either case, the members hesitated to be in the fraternity house by themselves for any period of time when the house was occupied. The story has stuck around campus, usually being told to fraternity rushes on their first week of school on campus or shared among students during homecoming weekend.

Another variation of the story has the entire ordeal occurring during the Little 500 festivities in the 1960s, leaving out any connection with the University of Iowa Hawks. Other versions say that Michael had his head blown off by an actual cannon ball instead of shrapnel from a cannon that backfires as in the story written above. So it begs the question, is this story true? In my opinion, it is nothing more than a unique urban legend to take place on Indiana University's campus. It remains to be a compelling story for students, and endures as a grim reminder of what could go wrong during celebrations on campus.

DORSON NEVER LEFT

A pivotal pillar of Indiana University's Folklore Institute is the late Professor Richard Dorson, who is still revered within the department. As a 1942 doctoral graduate of History from Harvard University, Richard Dorson went on to create the first folklore department and institute after he accepted his position at Indiana University in 1957. He is known as the "father of American folklore" and has influenced all those students and professors who study and teach in the curriculum now, so it is fitting that Richard Dorson would become the center of his own ghost story after death…

Illustrious History

It has been rumored for years that the Folklore and Ethnomusicology institute offices on North Fess Avenue are haunted. The Folklore Department is dedicated to the study of expressive culture through oral tales, customs, legends, jokes, and other popular beliefs. Meanwhile, the Ethnomusicology Department studies how culture is conveyed through dance, song, and music. Ghost stories and urban legends are popular topics within the Folklore and Ethnomusicology departments with professors and graduate students devoted to understanding the nature of these stories through the human condition. When the Ghost Walks were still held by the department, curious students and residents of Bloomington would gather at the front steps of the offices where they would be introduced to the first story of the night: *the ghost of the Folklore office*.

However, before diving into the ghosts of the Folklore Institute, it is important to know why they have hung around. The study of folklore as a topic of research started as far back as the 1920s by a group of professors from other departments, mainly the Anthropology, History, and English departments. Stith Thompson, a professor of English, started leading summer institutes on the topic in the 1940s, which continued into the 1960s. Because of their popularity, the summer institutes eventually gave rise to what we now know today at the Folklore Institute and Ethnomusicology Institute.

Warren Roberts, under the tutelage of Professor Thompson, was the first person to be awarded a degree in folklore in the United States in 1953. Three years later Professor Dorson arrived at the campus to lead and organize the rising folklore department along with Professor Thompson. In 1962, the Folklore and Ethnomusicology Institute was officially formed, led by Professor Dorson (who chaired the department from 1962-1981) and Professor Thompson. Professor Warren Roberts later joined the faculty, and all three men taught at the school until their deaths. These men have been celebrated within the Indiana University Folklore Institute and at other universities because, without them, the study of folklore as a serious subject would not have happened when it did. Indiana University was the first American university to establish a folklore department and since then all college folklore departments have been formed by graduates of Indiana University.

The Sightings Start

After Professor Dorson's death in 1981, odd things began to occur around the institute's offices. According to some student accounts, passersby to the building late at night would report seeing a man standing at an upstairs window looking down at the street when no one was supposedly in the offices. In other stories, secretaries who have worked for both the Ethnomusicology and Folklore offices have arrived early in the morning to find the faucets upstairs turned on and running at full force.

There also has been talk about the mysterious lamp pole set near the main entrance to the Folklore and Ethnomusicology Institute. For a long time after Professor Dorson's death, the lamp seemed to refuse to turn off. Day and night...this lamp remained lit. It wasn't until many years had passed before the bulb just seemed to give up. IU service crews came by one year to update the wiring in the area to make way for new streetlights and, according to rumor, cut power to that pole, but it wasn't long after that the lamp mysteriously turned back on again. This was completely unexplained since, according to official records, no electricity was being fed to it. Eventually the lamp dimmed again...and has remained off ever since.

At this point, it seems fair to ask the question: why is it believed that Professor Dorson haunts the Folklore offices and not one of the other important faculty members who have graced the halls of the institute? The reason is because faculty members have caught glimpses of Professor Dorson's wandering ghost. According to one account, in the spring of 1982 a graduate student was sitting in the Folklore office talking to a fellow staff member when she happened to glance outside the window they were positioned next to. What she saw shocked her — walking through the courtyard was the unmistakable form of Professor Dorson! The story goes that the graduate student recognized the figure as the late professor by two particular attributes: the distinct way he walked and the clothing he was wearing — a tweed jacket with elbow patches, not something commonly worn at the time. The graduate student called to her companion that

Richard Dorson was walking around outside; however, when the staff member peered out the window, no one was there. The graduate student then ran outside to look for the ghost to confirm what she saw, but she was unable to find him.

Another account of Dorson's ghost was made four years after he passed away...in a fellow faculty member's dream. In this account, Dorson instructed his "dreaming" colleague to deliver an important message in an attempt to solve the world's problems. Dorson's ghost appeared in a tennis outfit, over which he was wearing a long raincoat. These are important details since Dorson had fallen into a coma while playing tennis with his son in the spring of 1981 and passed away that fall. When the faculty member had an opportunity to speak to an audience at the Indiana University Auditorium later that year, he did send a message of being responsible in the fieldwork being done by future folklorists. Although not exactly advice on how to make the world a better place, it is good advice to keep stories from being "tainted" by lax fieldwork.

One of the stranger sightings of Professor Dorson is filed at the department, along with the many other reports collected about him. In this particular report which was made soon after his death, Professor Dorson had been seen riding in the backseat of a black Cadillac in Boise, Idaho. However, the reason as to why Dorson was seen out in Boise, Idaho, has never been explained. Was the black Cadillac supposed to be a hearse? No one knows.

Reflections

The faculty and staff of the present Folklore and Ethnomusicology Institute embrace their beloved ghost as a way of keeping those who helped form the department in their minds. With the hustle and bustle of the school year, it is easy to forget just how the department started and whom they owe this great opportunity to. Those who work in the Folklore and Ethnomusicology department on Indiana University's campus strive to preserve the rituals and special folktales of people all over the world. By working with other departments around campus, students and faculty of the Folklore Institute have been able to go out into the field and collect more and more stories from around the world. From folktales to urban legends, these stories tell us much about human nature. Maybe it is because the faculty has continued with the work he left behind that Professor Dorson returns to the department to observe. Professor Dorson's ghost has never hurt anyone, and he seems to be as much loved now in death as he was in life.

INDIANA'S GHOST TOWER

Without a doubt, the heartbeat of Indiana University is the towering structure known as the Indiana Memorial Union. Simply called the IMU for short by the university body, it boasts to be one of the largest student union buildings in the world. At a staggering 500,000 square feet, it houses ten floors with restaurants, cafes, study lounges, meeting rooms, the main IU bookstore, a hair salon, a bowling alley, a pool room, the Whittenberger Auditorium, and the Biddle Hotel...*as well as a host of Hoosier ghosts.*

Haunted History

The Indiana Union Board was established in 1909 by student John Whittenberger and past Indiana University President William Lowe Bryan, with the Indiana Memorial Union eventually created as a space where all members of the university could work together without tension. During this time, Indiana University had issues with members of the student body fighting amongst themselves. Fraternities, independents, sophomores, and freshmen were all in conflict with one another, so the Union Board was formed. Because of their achievements and contribution to the university, these two gentlemen are the namesakes of the previously mentioned Whittenberger Auditorium, the movie theater located on the first floor of the IMU, and the Bryan Room.

Although plans had been around since the beginning of the nineteenth century for a union building on campus, the IMU wasn't built until 1932. In 1952, after a year of intense debate, the Union Board and the Association of Women Studies merged. This meant that for the first time in the university's history women were admitted as members of the Union Board, the committee that organized so many of the university's student events.

In 1960, a hotel and conference center was added to the east side of the building, the Biddle Continuation Center. Named after the first director of the IMU, Ward Gray Biddle, the expansion includes 186 guest rooms in addition to a group of conference rooms known as the Tree Suites. Today it is quite common to see student social groups, academic conferences, and wedding receptions all occurring at the IMU at one time.

During the quiet hours between 2 and 6 a.m., when all the students have left and the guests are asleep in their beds, the maintenance staff is hard at work. It is also when they have experienced some odd — *maybe even paranormal* —activity in the building. Staff members have reported the sounds of footsteps following them around the halls, out of place smells, sounds of jovial laughter floating through the air, furniture being moved about the

The Indiana Memorial Union's West Tower has been marked by tragedy through the years. *Illustration by Liz Fuller.*

rooms, cold spots, voices talking, staffers' names being shouted from the hallways when they are alone in the corridor, and lights turning on and off by themselves. They have also seen what has been described as a black ghost dog patrolling the hallways inside the building and the sidewalks directly outside the main entrance. Phantom growling has also been heard before seeing the ghost dog, but why it haunts the IMU is unknown.

The most terrifying haunts to occur in the IMU are the residual specters of individuals who have jumped off of the West Tower. Visitors, students, and faculty have all reported witnessing figures jumping off the top of the tower, screaming as they plummet downward…only to *disappear* before hitting the second floor north patio. Stories around campus tell of cold spots and a displaced feeling of sadness on the patio where many people have landed after falling to their deaths.

The Bryan Room

According to staff, the West Wing, which is the older half of the building, has much more paranormal activity than the newer East Wing. One of the hotspots is the previously mentioned Bryan Room located on the eighth floor of the old tower on the West Wing. Janitors who clean up the IMU nightly turn off the lights once they are finished with the area —only to find them on again as they exit the building at the end of their rounds! IMU office staffers have experienced the same phenomenon… *the Bryan Room just refuses to be kept in the dark!*

The Bryan Room has a grizzly legend associated with it. The old west wing of the IMU used to be the location of the campus hotel before the Biddle Hotel expansion was added in 1960 and, according to legend, while it was still a hotel, a gentleman who had checked into a room on the fifth floor made his way up to the eighth floor and jumped out of the Bryan Room windows to his death. Perhaps this is why the lights always remain on or why the west wing elevator has the peculiar habit of stopping at the fifth floor without being prompted…perhaps the ghost of the gentleman is repeating the events of that night.

The Tudor Room

A popular restaurant and meeting place in the IMU is the Tudor Room, but few guests know of its resident spirit named "Jacob." In the dining room, there is a painting of a young boy holding a pumpkin hanging among the large medieval tapestries adorning the walls. The painting is entitled "Halloween" by O. O. Haig, and its subject is assumed to be Jacob, a young child who died in a fire just after the painting was finished.

A few years ago, when the tapestries were taken down for cleaning, Jacob supposedly threw a fit and repeatedly sent the table dressings in disarray during the night. Tudor Room staff had a hard time maintaining the image of the dining room while the tapestries were away due to the nightly raids against their table settings. Chairs would be moved around the room as well, adding to the chaos. However, once the tapestries were returned to their home in the Tudor Room, all of the unexplained activity ceased.

You don't have to walk far to get to the next location where a ghost has been seen in the IMU. Just open the main doors of the Tudor Room and step out into the hallway…if you are lucky, you will run into the phantom pregnant woman. She is said to pace along that long corridor at night looking agitated. However, when a curious observer approaches her, she suddenly disappears into thin air. One of the IMU's more elusive apparitions to catch a glimpse of, the reasons why she remains there are unknown.

The Federal Room

Located on the third floor, it is modeled in the style of Colonial Williamsburg. If you happen to be in the Federal Room for a banquet or other social event, you may notice the unfinished painting of Mary Burney, which has stirred up its own ghostly tale. An art critic in life, Burney disliked the portrait being painted of her. However, before it could be finished, Burney passed away. What resulted was this unfinished painting, which was hung in the Federal Room regardless of the state it was in. This act seems to have stirred the sleeping spirit of Mary Burney, whose signature perfume has been detected lingering around the room from time to time in front of the painting.

Resting on either side of Mary Burney's painting are the urns of her late husband and son who mysteriously died in a fire before her death. A mystery developed some years ago when one of the urns disappeared and was not found for many years. One day, when the Federal Room was opened for an event, the prodigal urn was found sitting besides the painting — and it has been in that place ever since.

The Tree Suites

Located on the second floor of the east wing are the Tree Suites, a cluster of meeting rooms set aside for conferences or student club activities. To get to the Tree Suites, you have to walk through the student lounge located on the second floor, passing the elevators and a large marble staircase to the first floor. This area is home to a male ghost that has been seen from time-to-time walking through late at night. Legend has it that a man in a three-piece suit has been known to haunt that staircase and corridor of rooms after he committed suicide in the building, perhaps in the Biddle Hotel. Pictures taken of the central staircase have shown a shadowy ghost standing on the landing beneath the portrait of past Indiana University President and Chancellor Herman B. Wells.

What is remarkable is that while I was a student at IU, I have *seen* this Tree Suites Ghost. One Friday night in the fall of 2006, around 10 p.m., I was walking with my friends from the Trees Suites after a social event on the second floor. When my group reached the stairwell, I remember looking down to the landing before taking a step down the staircase — and I *saw* a man in a three-piece gray suit looking back up at us, watching as the group of students quickly approached him. He looked to be in his mid-50s,

Taken in January 2009, this photo shows a strange glowing anomaly floating in the air. Although many photography experts have looked at the photo, no explanation can be found. Is this evidence of the paranormal?

but he disappeared from sight just as quickly as he had appeared. To my disappointment, I was the only one who happened to see the ghost.

The Investigation

Members of the Indiana Ghost Trackers Bloomington Chapter have been allowed access to the IMU in order to investigate the alleged haunts within the building. They investigated the same area in 2003 and 2005 and, according to their report, the Bryan Room proved to be the most active. From that room, they caught two EVP clips and witnessed a chair move by itself during the EVP session.

Reflections

The Indiana Memorial Union has continued to be the social center of the campus for nearly a century. From the beginning, the IMU's location has made it the melting pot of campus culture. Perhaps because of this it has become a place where students can swap ghost stories and legends, and this could possibly explain why the IMU has transformed into a center of paranormal phenomenon. The known death to occur on the site, mixing with urban legends provided by the student body, has created a plethora of ghosts haunting the huge building. The intelligent ghosts within the IMU do not seem harmful, but rather look at the current campus student body in curiosity.

THE SPOOKS OF READ HALL

Every university has a "haunted" dormitory or two since that is where students spend a majority of their time doing homework, cramming for tests, and hanging out with friends, but within every dormitory are those dark places where students are hesitant to go…the stairwells with flickering light bulbs and those laundry rooms with questionable odors. Some dorm rooms just never feel completely hospitable to the residents. Read Hall, like so many other dormitories, has those dark stories from the past that on dreary days around Halloween are brought out of hiding and shared among the new class.

The History

The residence hall built on the corner of Jordan Avenue and Jones Road was dedicated in 1955 as Smithwood Hall. In 1962, it was renamed to honor Professor Daniel Read who had taught at the school during its early frontier days. Conveniently located between the Jacobs School of Music, the Musical Arts Center, and School of Education, Read Hall houses many of the music and education majors residing on campus. The X-shaped tower made of Indiana limestone has four wings — Beck, Curry, Clark, and Landes — that houses both male and female students. Male students live in the Beck and Curry wings while the female students reside in the Clark and Landes wings, though this setup has been known to change through the years. Read has a traditional university dorm ambiance, with a feeling of calm permeating its hallways and student lounges. Behind this veil of serenity, though, lies two tales of collegiate terror…

The Girl in the Yellow Dress

As the story goes, before the dormitory became known as Read Hall, there was a volatile young couple that met and fell in love while studying on campus. Although they loved each other dearly, they were prone to very angry and intense arguments. The legend never states what the girl majored in or even what her name was, but it was rumored that she was a beautiful girl of seventeen with gorgeous long black hair. Her boyfriend has never been named either, but it has been said that he was a pre-med student who lived on the third floor of Read Hall.

One night the couple attended a social event at which the girl wore a lovely yellow dress. Although they left for the event as a happy couple, they returned shortly after in a heated argument. What started the fight is unknown, but the fiery exchange of words followed them into the boy-

The "Girl in the Yellow Dress" is one of two reported ghosts roaming the halls of Read Dormitory. *Illustration by Kat Klockow.*

friend's dorm room and was loud enough to keep curious onlookers at bay. It is said that in a fit of rage the young med student did the unthinkable: grabbing a scalpel, he slashed his girlfriend's neck. Panicking and gasping for air with an exposed trachea, the young girl stumbled around the room after the boy until she fell over…dead. The story takes a gory turn in one version — overcome with grief over his murderous action, the young man surgically removes her beautiful face and stores it in his dresser drawer — but all variations agree that the young man then moved the bloody corpse of his girlfriend into the basement tunnel system near the laundry room.

It was not long before the murder was discovered and the young man was arrested. Some variations of the story state that the boyfriend was thrown in jail. Another states that he was put into an insane asylum (perhaps the notorious Central State Hospital in Indianapolis, which is also reportedly haunted) while other versions state that he hanged himself in grief. Although the young girl's body was buried, it seems this tragic co-ed does not rest in peace. Since the 1960s, there have been reports made by students of seeing the blood-stained apparition of a girl in a yellow dress floating along the hallways of the third floor. Perhaps she is looking for her face, which was so heinously cut from her body. In one report from the 1970s, a male student was studying in his dorm room when he felt a cold chill come over him. When he turned around to find the source of the chilly atmosphere, he came face-to-face with the ghost of the Girl in Yellow! She had been standing behind him watching him work away. As soon as the student saw her, she evaporated into a mist and the room's temperature returned to normal.

Students have also reported electrical problems on the third floor, especially concerning stereos. The Girl in Yellow is suspected of raising the music to a deafening volume with her unseen hands, and "she" has also been seen roaming the dim laundry areas near where her body was dumped. There, she has appeared with no face…only her blood-soaked hair dangles over the gaping hole left behind. Students are leery about traveling to the laundry room or walking the third-floor halls past midnight for fear of meeting her horrid apparition in person.

December Remembered

There is a second, less threatening ghost that travels on the sixth floor. She is simply known as "Paula" and was a resident assistant (or RA for short) in the late 1980s. As the legend goes, shortly after finals one semester, Paula received the news that she had possibly failed one of her classes. If this was truly the case, this put her job as an RA in jeopardy, which in turn would have resulted in her leaving school due to financial problems. Distraught and panicking alone in her room, Paula decided that ending her life was the most sensible option. Not pausing to rethink her decision, Paula threw herself down the sixth floor staircase, breaking her neck and dying alone on the cold staircase landing.

Since then her ghost has repeated its fatal fall every midnight on December 12th, the anniversary of her death. Students and staff who have been on the floor on that night have heard thumping and Paula's last shrill scream on that particular night. Odd sensations — such as cold spots and the feeling of being watched — have been reported on the sixth floor female wings of Landes and Clark. One student reported waking up to find a shadowy person standing at her doorway one morning. She got up quickly to see who it was, but the apparition quickly faded into thin air. Shortly after the incident, the female student was shocked to learn about Paula's story and assumed it was Paula who she had seen.

When I lived on campus, I heard from a friend a story involving the ghost of Paula. She had told me that a student woke up in the middle of the night to find someone using the adjoining bathroom to her suite on the sixth floor. Unlike the other floors of the dormitory, the sixth floor has single-occupant rooms that are joined together by a shared bathroom. Usually this would be no reason for alarm...except that this girl *didn't* have a suite mate!

Reflections

The stories from Read Hall have captivated the imaginations of university students for decades. The Girl in Yellow has become a ghostly celebrity of sorts every Halloween when her legend is printed in the school's newspaper along with stories about Paula, Portico's Restaurant, and the "Good Doctor" of the Career Development Center. Like other paranormal hopefuls, I too have waited to watch Paula fall down the staircase at the stroke of midnight on December 12th. The funny thing is, no one seems to know which staircase Paula fell down. So for those few who believe that Paula's residual ghost does fall down the stairs, it is a hard decision to pick which staircase to wait at. This results in some parties breaking up to wait in each stairwell for something to happen.

However, I will point out that no record of a girl named Paula committing suicide in Read Residence Hall has ever been found, nor has any documentation of a murder in the 1960s. The first murders ever to occur on campus of current students didn't take place until 1992 and those occurred in the Eigenmann Residence Center. Even though the stories turned out not to be true, these two spirits live on in the minds of IU students. In a way, these stories bring a little bit of the paranormal into the students' everyday lives...is that really a bad thing?

CHILLS AT DUNN CEMETERY

When visitors to Indiana University stroll the university, they run into the chilling site of Dunn Cemetery in the middle of campus. Some students think the cemetery is a cool reminder of those who came before the University while other students think the cemetery is creepy…an unnecessary reminder of our own mortality. Usually the first question out of a visitor's mouth is, "Why is there a cemetery here?" The answer is simple: the University is obligated to keep it there.

Morbid History

Indiana University wouldn't be the internationally recognized university it is today without the land it was built on. Moses F. Dunn was a landowner and farmer in the 1800s whose family had been in the Bloomington area for generations. His farm stood where the university stands now, and like many farming families in the early days of Indiana's history, they had a cemetery located on their land.

In 1855, George Grundy Dunn deeded the land that the cemetery is on for the "perpetual use as a cemetery" to the decedents of three Brewster sisters: Agness B. Alexander, Ellinor Dunn, and Jennet Irving. These women played an important role in Bloomington's history, being some of the first families to settle the area in the early 1800s. Between 1830 and 1841, the sisters passed away and were laid to rest in Dunn Cemetery under one large headstone that still stands today.

In 1883, Moses F. Dunn sold the old family land to the university in a large land grant; the purchase included the cemetery. In the land grant agreement that was made over a hundred years ago the university promised to keep the cemetery as well as a special set of trees intact. One of those trees is located in the cemetery and the other is in the courtyard of the chemistry building. The cemetery still stands…with the university growing around it.

The cemetery was a part of the original homestead of Samuel Dunn II; the Dunn family farmhouse stood where the current HPER building now stands. Dunn Cemetery is still in use, and the most recent burial among the gravestones took place in 2004. The first person buried within the cemetery walls is that of seventeen-year-old Jennet Seward, a granddaughter of Jennet Brewster Irvin. Ms. Seward died in 1814 from massive head trauma after hitting her head on a wagon wheel. However, Jennet Seward's grave is *not* marked within the cemetery. Currently there are sixty-eight relatives buried in the cemetery with room for an additional twenty-five internments. There are 287 heirs living who can be buried in the cemetery. To be interned in Dunn Cemetery, one must have documentation that he

Beck Chapel has been the scene of many happy memories for IU students and alumni. *Illustration by Liz Fuller.*

or she is a member of the Brewster-Dunn clan. There are two exceptions to this burial rule — Dr. Frank O. Beck and his wife Daisy. Dr. Frank Beck and his wife are the namesakes of Beck Chapel, the small nondenominational, nonsectarian chapel located within the cemetery's walls.

How the Becks became buried in the cemetery is an interesting story. It started in 1956 when Dr. Beck desired to have a nondenominational chapel built on the university's campus, but this was forbidden due to the country's separation of church-and-state doctrine. One decedent of the Brewster sisters, Curtis D. Aiken, who worked at the university, began talking to Dr. Beck and soon the two became friends. After a vote of the relatives responsible for the management of the cemetery, the family allowed the chapel to be built on land once set aside for a 'dead house' (aka a mausoleum). At the same time, the family also allowed Dr. Beck and his wife Daisy to be buried next to the chapel that they helped build.

Dunn Cemetery is actually one of two cemeteries on the IU campus. The other cemetery is Rogers Cemetery, which is located at Foster Quadrangle off of Fee Lane on the northeast side of the campus. Unlike Dunn Cemetery, Rogers Cemetery has no paranormal activity associated with it, although a few students have been unnerved by the cemetery's presence. The Rogers Cemetery is a separate family's cemetery, with the land around it purchased after the Dunn homestead was in order for the university to expand. Both the Dunn and Rogers cemeteries are still owned by their respective families, although the University maintains the land.

Eerie Legends

Stories persist around campus that members of the Brewster and Dunn families may not entirely rest in peace in the small cemetery. There have been reports of a figure dressed in a black robe gliding along the headstones in Dunn Cemetery. Who is the figure in black robes? Why does it continue to appear in the cemetery? No one seems to know when the figure first started showing up in the cemetery.

Students walking through the campus in the witching hours of the night have claimed to hear sounds of babies or children crying coming from the cemetery, but when they approach the cemetery to find the cause of the sounds, the crying suddenly stops. The same crying sounds have been reported along the Jordan River in the vicinity of the cemetery; again, when approached, the sounds cease. Although reports of the paranormal are scarce in the old cemetery, these stories are well-known and widespread among students living on campus.

Reflections

Are these stories just campus urban legends or real accounts from past students? When interviewed, many alumni and students could tell me the various stories associated with the cemetery, but *no one* personally knew of anyone who had experienced these paranormal events firsthand. Although the stories of paranormal encounters in Dunn Cemetery are incredible, they may be just that...stories. Whether the cemetery is haunted or not, it serves a reminder to the university community of where the school's roots come from. The cemetery also stands as a reminder that there are many generations of students and residents who have lived and thrived on the very land that they reside today.

IU'S MYSTERY TUNNELS

One of the most mysterious locations on Indiana University's campus is below the streets where students tread: the IU tunnel system. There are many rumors circulating around the student body about where the tunnel system leads because it is one area that students rarely ever see while on campus. Rumors about dead bodies, bizarre rituals, and twisted places have transformed this restricted area of campus into a fun house of horrors.

Restricted History

It is true that many of the buildings around Indiana University Bloomington's campus are linked together by a maze of tunnels, but just how easy it is to access these tunnels is a whole different story. As the campus grew, so has this labyrinth of service tunnels under the streets. Some are large enough to walk through while others resemble steam tubes. Today they are how the university is wired; electric, gas, and Ethernet cables run through these tunnels in order to serve the needs of the various departments. Although guided access from time to time has been given to journalists of the university's newspaper *The Indiana Daily Student*, these tunnels are restricted to all unauthorized personnel. This of course hasn't kept the curious from prying....

Dead Bodies

Our fist legend regarding the underground tunnel system dates back to the late nineteenth century when transit via the railroad was far more frequent. Central Indiana was a hub of train activity since many of the railroads that connected Chicago to Cincinnati ran through the area. As the story goes, an elephant was traveling through central Indiana with circus trainers when the train they were riding had an accident. The elephant perished, its body sent to Indiana University for research purposes. When it entered Bloomington, however, the body went missing. Rumor had it that ecologists who thought that the body could be preserved instead of being used for educational purposes had stolen the elephant's body, stashing it in IU's tunnel system in order to throw off the trail of the authorities. However, when they returned to retrieve the body, they couldn't remember how to get to it. Although curious personnel have looked around the tunnels from time to time, no elephant remains have ever been discovered in the miles of underground.

What is interesting about the story is that it has a glimmer of truth since the Gentry Brothers Circus did have its headquarters in downtown Bloomington. When the circus was still operational, their offices were located in the large building on Kirkwood Avenue that now houses the Irish Lion and Crazy Horse restaurants. The building was constructed in 1882 as a hotel, but also had adequate room for offices, which the Gentry Brothers Circus Company occupied until they were purchased by P.T. Barnum's Circus Company. It could be possible that one of their animals died and was donated to the University for study, but how any ecology activist could get the body of an elephant into the tunnel system is beyond comprehension since the entrances are very small.

Fatal Hazing

Another account concerns fraternity initiation rituals in the tunnels around North Jordan Avenue. According to the stories, one year a pledge was accidentally killed while participating in an unnamed fraternity's hazing. How the pledge dies varies from story-to-story; some say he died due to alcohol poisoning, others say he was beaten to death, and others still say he was strangled.

Reports of real fraternity or sorority pledges dying in initiations or other related events have occurred in the news in recent years around the United States. Indiana University is not immune to these tragedies, with deaths related to Greek Life activities occurring in 2001 and 2007. However, no deaths have ever occurred in the underground tunnels on campus. This is due to that fact that by the time the tunnels reach the North Jordan area, they are simply too small to conduct any such ritual.

Reflections

Whatever the cause, some interesting things have been reported to haunt or be in the underground tunnel system at Indiana University. Whether it be paranormal, zoological, or just a variation of an old urban legend, these stories are spread to amuse its audiences. I would not suggest that anyone go looking for anything down in the tunnel system however…it's hot, it smells, and once you enter you may not be able to find your way out. Always remember, safety first!

MARRED BY TRAGEDY

Bloomington's Suicide Tower

Rising high from the thick forest of trees on Bloomington's campus is the enormous ten-story building known as Ballantine Hall. A center for academics for many of the students, it has remained an important landmark on IU's campus for more than fifty years. For all the happy memories created in this building, though, there is a darker side of shadow and despair, as some people believe the ghosts of Bloomington's past walk the halls, reliving their feelings of failure and despair.

Hidden History

Built in 1959, the building was named after Elisha Ballantine, one of the first professors to teach at Indiana University in 1854. While still a modest state university, Elisha Ballantine taught both mathematics and ancient modern languages to the first few generations of graduates. Ballantine later became the chairman of the language department and vice president of the college between the years of 1884 and 1886. For a brief stint of his academic career, Ballantine was the acting university president. This happened in 1884 after Lemuel Moss, the sixth president of Indiana University, abruptly resigned his position. Ballantine, as the vice president, stepped in to take control of the office until fellow IU professor David Starr Jordan was appointed as the seventh college president.

Ballantine Hall once held the record for being the largest academic building ever on a college campus in the world. Though no longer the world's largest academic building, it still hosts quite a variety of subjects within its walls. While I was on campus, most of my math and language classes were held in Ballantine, along with a mix of archeology and literature courses. The building is also known for being the site where the formula for fluoride was invented, so the school does receive modest royalties for the discovery. Contrary to rumors, however, Ballantine Hall was not built with the money from the formula.

Few people know that before Ballantine Hall was built, the site was home to a collection of fraternity, sorority, and boarding houses collectively called Forest Place. One of the buildings razed for the construction of Ballantine Hall was Alpha Hall, the campus's first women's dormitory built in 1906. Alpha Hall was originally privately owned and operated, but was leased to the university in 1919 and eventually purchased in 1936. In 1961, the old residence hall was outdated and no longer needed; it was demolished so construction of the new hall could begin.

Ballantine Hall is primarily used for classrooms and faculty offices. The top floors (five through ten) are used as offices for a variety of departments while the first four floors are dedicated to a mix of classrooms, lecture halls, and language labs. One of the notable items on display in Ballantine Hall is the six-foot diameter globe in the lobby of the first floor. Two alumni donated this globe back in 1961. Located along the north hallway on the first floor is also a set of temple rubbings from Thailand that depict the *Ramakien*, Thailand's national epic story.

Supernatural Sightings

Thousands of people walk through Ballantine Hall on a daily basis, unaware of the horrible past events that have occurred on the premises. For many people on campus, Ballantine Halls has the grim nickname of the "suicide tower." It's a deserving name, regrettably, since the entire history of the building has been marked by the tragedy of suicide. Most of the suicides occurred off of the eighth or ninth floor: a 28-year-old graduate student plunged to his death in 1970 from the eighth floor. In August of 1999, a forty-year-old man jumped from a ninth floor hallway window. In November of 2000, a twenty-year-old male student plunged to his death from a south facing eighth-story window. These are just a few accounts recorded in articles from the *Herald Times*.

Not all attempts from the top of Ballantine Hall end in tragedy, however. In April 2004, a 22-year-old male student who had withdrawn from Indiana University attempted to take his life from the eighth floor of the hall. After breaking through the windows with a wooden chair, the man jumped through the north facing windows, only to fall onto an awning covering the north doors on the second floor of the building. The man survived, albeit with two broken legs. Since he jumped right before noon — the time when many students are walking to their classes — several students, myself included, witnessed his fall.

Naturally, due to the atmosphere that surrounds the building, there are rumors that its halls are haunted. An Indiana University security officer reported this account in 2005:

He was making his rounds around 9 or 10 p.m. on the fifth floor when suddenly many of the doors in the hallway began to shake violently, as if somebody was trying to desperately escape from the rooms. Thinking that someone was locked in, the officer opened the door nearest to him…only to find it empty and silent. A few doors down a professor was working in his office; the security officer approached him about the doors rattling. Baffled after hearing the security officer's story, the professor replied that it had been quiet all night on the floor and that he was the last faculty member left in the offices that day. Puzzled, the officer thanked the professor and went on with his watch, completely bewildered by the fact he was the only person to experience the phenomenon that night.

The security officer's account helps to support reports of unexplained activity in Ballantine Hall made by other employees.

According to maintenance staff working in the building, there is a spectral janitor who has been seen working on the fifth floor late at night. This specter seems solid to those who have witnessed it, but when they approach the "janitor"…he vanishes into thin air. More than one staff member has described the same specter — even if their reports are years apart.

Tenth Floor Haunts

According to the maintenance staff, another paranormal hotspot is the entire tenth floor of Ballantine Hall, where they have reported seeing *orbs dancing* along the darkened hallways.

Other reports describe unexplainable flashes of light streaking before the staff member's eyes. Some members of the maintenance staff have allegedly refused to clean the top floor after midnight while others are hesitant to work the floor alone.

Reflections

There are many questions that come up on the subject of the haunting of Ballantine Hall. Like the Indiana Memorial Union, Ballantine holds a dark impression within its walls that few people notice. Because the building has stood witness to many suicides through the decades, perhaps it has now become a place where the ghosts of victims past have come to gather. Questions arise about the specters, though: Who would want to haunt their last known place on earth? Why would an old janitor haunt the fifth floor of the hall? What have the staff seen on the tenth floor numerous times that seems to have scared the daylights out of them? Perhaps the spirits that haunt Ballantine Hall have been there since the location was Forest Place… perhaps they are older than we know.

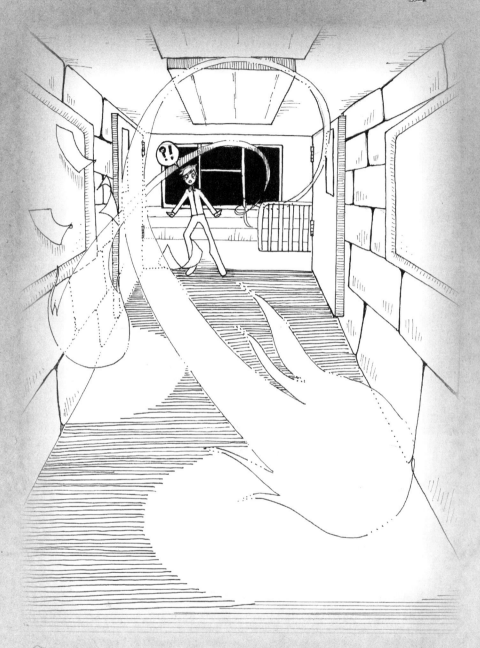

Maintenance staff working late at night in Ballantine Hall has reported seeing strange orbs of light dancing around the tenth floor. *Illustration by Kat Klockow.*

Eigenmann's Spook Tower

Eigenmann Residence Center, also known as Eigenmann Hall or just Eigenmann, is one of the tallest buildings on IU's campus; it's also the tallest residence hall on campus. However, like Ballentine Hall and the Indiana Memorial Union, its height attracts those who desire to end their lives. The dormitory, for only being a few decades old, has a dark history of murder and suicide.

A Dark History

Construction on Eigenmann Hall started in 1968 at 10th and North Union streets. The hall was designed by the New York architectural firm Eggers and Higgins to house graduate students and older (over 21 years of age) international students who were studying on campus. In 1998, however, the residency requirement was repealed and undergraduate students, American or international, could live there. Many of my friends stayed here, and today the resident population continues to be a mix of graduate and undergraduate students.

The residence hall is named in honor of Carl Eigenmann, who most students may not know. He was a famous ichthyologist [Ichthyology is a branch of zoology, the study of fish] who was born in Flehingen, Germany, in 1863. He led a globe-trekking life, graduating with a bachelor's degree from Indiana University in 1886, and he is mostly remembered for two things: his work with his wife, fellow biologist Rosa Smith Eigenmann — together, they described many of the North and South American fish for the first time — and becoming IU's Dean of Graduate Studies in 1908. Through his years of active study, Eigenmann discovered over 120 new species of fish, twenty-eight new genuses of fish, and documented the blindfish and salamanders in the caves of Indiana, Texas, Missouri, and Cuba. On April 25, 1927 Carl Eigenmann passed away at his home in San Diego; he was sixty-four years old.

Through the years Eigenmann Hall has received numerous nicknames. Because the dormitory had such strict quiet hours, the residents often called the building "Eigetraz." Another nickname the building was known by in the past was "Tokyo Tower" due to the large population of Asian international students residing there. However, the darkest title given to the building is "suicide tower," due to the many suicides that occurred within the building and off of its roof.

The dormitory was also the site of the first murders of current students on campus grounds...an honor many who work there would like to pass up. On April 23, 1992, graduate student Susan Clements and friend Steven Molen were shot to death on the fourteenth floor of

Eigenmann Hall by Susan's ex-boyfriend turned stalker Andreas Drexler. After shooting the pair in Eigenmann, Drexler fled from the dormitory to his car a few blocks away. That same day, before the authorities could arrest him, Drexler committed suicide in his car, which was filled with 2,000 rounds of ammunition, a hunting knife, three gasoline cans, and a Bible. Due to the location of the murders and the manner in which they were performed, this tragedy became nationally, maybe even internationally, known. The campus and university mourned the loss of Clements and Molen and questioned how such a horrible thing could happen on such a safe campus. Because it took much of the sense of innocence and safety away from campus life, the wounds of this incident have never fully healed.

Sad Suicide Tales

Since 1970, other more private tragedies have taken place. Debbie, from the Class of 1976, lived in Eigenmann Hall during the first years of its operation. There were many memories of her years on campus, but she recalled one particularly tragic memory when I asked her about living at Eigenmann.

"There was an alarm that kept going off," Debbie started. This is a fairly common experience in a dormitory full of students. "It was on the eighth floor where I lived, and after while others complained to the RA [resident assistant] to do something about it."

Debbie's face sank while recalling the second part of the story:

 "The RA entered the room to turn off the alarm clock, but found the student who lived there rolled up in blankets and a sleeping bag—dead."

From the reports that filtered through the student body, a gun had been found among the blankets with the student. The girl had rolled herself up into the blankets and sleeping bag to muffle the sound of the gun going off when she shot herself in the head. Now why the student, who was an international graduate student from Korea, would do such a thing is complete speculation.

Debbie, trying to reason so many years later why anyone would choose to commit suicide, suggested that the student didn't do well in school and succumbed to pressure. Perhaps this is so, since academics are taken far more seriously outside the United States, especially in Asian countries such as China, Korea, and Japan.

Giving in to academic pressure seems to be a common factor in many of the "suicide stories" from Eigenmann. Debbie also mentioned an incident where a Japanese graduate student jumped from her fourteenth-story window to her death because she did poorly in school. She reportedly did this, said Debbie, "to keep her family's honor." Although committing suicide to keep the family's honor, known as seppuku or hara-kiri, was an occurrence during the samurai dominated years of Japan's history so samurai would not fall into enemy hands via ceremonial suicide, it rarely has been practiced since World War II.

 "The girl who touched her hands on the power station," Melanie started...

In this story provided by Melanie Hunter, the victim was again a Korean student. My interest was piqued because it was a new story about Eigenmann that I hadn't heard before.

 "She was from Korea, [and] she got a B instead of an A [in a course]. She got distraught...well, that's what I've heard."

Rob, Melanie's husband who was sitting next to her during the interview, nodded in agreement as she told the story. He remembered this happening too.

 "Dunn Street curves around, and she went to the power station and touched her hands to the box... It's said her hands melted into the power station."

Melanie shook her head while looking down at the carpeted floor. At the time of this event in the early 1980s, Melanie and Rob were living on campus and were affected when, as a result of the girl's action, the power went out on the whole north side of the campus.

~~~~~

Although not occurring in the building, there have been some incidents of students being hit by trains while crossing the train tracks across the street north of Eigenmann. As recently as 2008, there have been reports of students committing suicide by jumping in front of the trains that still frequently cross through the campus.

Haunting Accounts

Students living at the dormitory and even passersby have reported seeing dark, shadowy figures leaping from the rooftop...only to disappear before impacting the ground. Perhaps this is the residual haunting of the Japanese student mentioned earlier? Or is it the culmination of all the residual energy of the victims' final moments? No one is sure.

After the Clements and Molen murders in 1992, odd occurrences have been reported from the fourteenth floor, including lights flickering without a reason, the feeling of being watched, and objects being moved. Residents and visitors to the dormitory have also experienced displaced emotions such as sadness or anger.

While working on her book *Haunted Halls: Ghostlore of American College Campuses*, Elizabeth Tucker toured the fourteenth floor with spiritual exorcist Barbara Lee. As the two walked along the hallway, Lee exclaimed that she had detected a student's spirit on the floor. According to Lee, the male student had jumped out of his dorm room window and was trying to push her out as well. They then walked past a room that had its door closed and Lee identified this room as the spirit's dorm room in life. She said that a spectral funeral wreath hung there now. The exorcist attempted to get the ghost to pass on into the afterlife...whether she was successful at the spiritual exorcism or not is difficult to tell.

Reflections

Eigenmann Residence Hall has certainly seen too many tragic events happen in and around its property. Murder, suicide, and loss... these are all things that have imprinted themselves into the dark history of this residence hall.

Stories of suicide coming from the residence hall tend to be about Asian women who decided suicide was the answer to their academic problems. One question often asked when looking at this is, why? A short answer from me, who used to live in Japan, is this: culturally, suicide is not as shameful like it is in many other countries. It does not carry the same stigma as it would in other cultures. While this is not a full answer, it may explain why Asian students seem to be the subject of so many of these reports. However, do keep in mind that they aren't the only ones choosing this path; both males and females of other nationalities have also chosen to end their lives in Eigenmann...I just couldn't find people who had encountered their spirits.

Most students living at Eigenmann today are largely unaware of the tragic events that have occurred in the place they now call home. Perhaps that is why the ghosts remain, to serve as eternal reminders or even warnings to the living of what the pressures of academia can drive people to do. Or could it be that the ghosts in Eigenmann remain confused about death as they were about life...and just can't seem to leave the last place they called home?

THE "GOOD DOCTOR"

One of the most known and talked about "haunted" locations on Indiana University's campus is the Career Development Center, otherwise known as the CDC. Three ghosts are said to make the old building their stomping grounds: the home's original owner, a young co-ed, and a gruesome gentleman referred to as the "Good Doctor." Located on the corner of North Jordan Avenue and 10th Street, the CDC sits across from the colossal Herman B. Wells Main Library. Hidden from 10th Street by massive trees and scrubs, this only adds to the eerie atmosphere around the CDC building. According to legends, the CDC has been haunted for a number of decades, perhaps even before the university purchased the land in 1944. Warning: The building's history is long, twisted, and not for the faint of heart!

Horrid History

It all began with the building's construction at the earlier part of the twentieth century. According to legend, the original owner contracted the house to be built out of a fit of insanity, but shortly after the home was finished, the gentleman committed suicide in the basement with a shot to the head from his pistol. Whether it was a moment of insanity that brought him to his end or the mounting debts for building such a large home as being the reason for his suicide has been lost to history. Nonetheless, the man thought it was best to end his life with a pull of a trigger.

After the death of the original owner, it is speculated that the land was purchased by the shifty "Good Doctor" to be used as his private residence and site of his private clinic. For years, the doctor treated residents of Bloomington in addition to the growing number of students residing on campus with their physical ailments. However, the Good Doctor had a grizzly secret: he performed illegal abortions on distraught and desperate co-eds from the campus and surrounding town who found themselves pregnant in an era when it was a serious social disgrace. At the time, abortions were illegal in the United States and society looked down on both the women and doctors involved in the procedure. Keeping this entirely secret was of the utmost importance for the doctor, so every night after a day of operations and procedures the doctor would throw the unborn fetuses and other "medical trash" into the home's coal shoot to be incinerated. As the stories go, the charred remains were then hidden within the floor or walls of the basement after they had cooled enough to be buried, much of it around the staircase.

According to legend, tragedy struck one night in the early 1940s when a young seventeen-year-old female patient came in to have one of the secret procedures. While performing the illegal abortion, the doctor accidentally nicked a vital artery and the patient bled to death on the operating table. In a panic, he stuffed her body down the coal shoot into the home's furnace and cleaned up the bloody mess around his operating room. Later he continued his nightly ritual of lighting the furnace and burning the medical waste inside the shoot.

However, the girl was missed by her family and friends and a missing person's report was submitted. It didn't take long for her trail to lead to and end at the doctor's house. Suspecting him of her murder, or perhaps the local law enforcement was relieved to find a reason to go after him, the Good Doctor was arrested. Being a wealthy citizen of the town, the doctor was able to make bail and returned to his home. Before any more of his secrets could be exposed and with his downfall quickly approaching, it is said that the Good Doctor climbed the spiral staircase in his home to the third floor, tied a noose around his neck, and stepped off. The fall snapped his neck instantly with the recoil of his fall. The authorities discovered his lifeless body when they came to question him about the girl's murder.

Eerie Experiences

Indiana University purchased the property and began leasing it out. One tenant was the Phi Kappa Tau Fraternity. Wishing to be located closer to campus (their previous residence being the Buskirk-Showers Mansion on North Walnut Street), the Phi Kappa Tau Fraternity rented the space. One year a fraternity member named Danny J. was the first person to move into the house. While unpacking his things on the second floor, he heard the distinct sound of footsteps walking down the spiral staircase. Perplexed about what he was hearing since he thought he was the only person in the house, Danny called out, possibly thinking it was a fellow fraternity member returning to campus early and unannounced. Approaching the staircase, Danny froze at the realization that he was definitely alone in the large house. Or was he? As he stood in the middle of the staircase trying to figure out what was going on, he felt a cold hand on his shoulder, which sent the young man into a seizure. His fellow fraternity brothers found him on the floor and rushed him to the medical building across the street.

That hasn't been the only experience to occur in the building. A later fraternity member reported running into a transparent fig-

The Career Development Center is known for two things on campus — its gradu-ate resources and its ghosts. *Illustration by Kat Klockow.*

ure of a man in the second floor bathroom washing blood off his hands. The fraternity member watched the ghost walk past him and briskly climb up the staircase...where the apparition evaporated into thin air! The fraternity member was baffled by what he had just witnessed.

Since the house has now been turned into a campus office, staff members have had their own run-ins with the home's ghosts. The ghost of the seventeen-year-old who died in the building has been seen wandering the second floor of the house. Staffers have some-times mistaken her as a current student...until she *fades away* into the air. The sounds of a female crying have also been reported on the second floor and in the basement without a source to be found.

The spiral staircase has been a focal point of many of the sight-ings and supernatural experiences. Not only has the apparition of the Good Doctor been witnessed climbing the stairwell, people have also seen his body swaying from the top of the staircase. Phantom footsteps have been heard and staff has reported being touched by a cold, unseen hand while climbing the staircase to the third floor.

Probably one of the most widely talked about phenomena to occur at the CDC is the sound of babies or children crying in the basement classroom. No apparitions have ever been said to be seen; however, cold spots have been reported, with some thinking that it may be the spirit of the original owner. Like the upper stories of the house, though, much of the activity has been said to take place around the staircase.

Oddities and Rituals

While the Phi Kappa Tau Fraternity was occupying the house, one of the rumored initiation rituals was a challenge to see how long the pledges could sit in the old coal shoot. After being told the house's grizzly history and the Good Doctor's deeds, the pledges were placed, one at a time, into the shoot with a single lit candle. If they could stand to be in the shoot for an extended period of time, they passed the challenge. If not, they didn't become a member.

There are also reports that a séance was held around the coal shoot. Allegedly, candles were placed in the coal bin and the flames rose to an astonishing foot high before flickering out. Was it because it was placed inside a coal shoot where the residue could have still been flammable or because the spirits of the dead were talking? We may never know.

The house boasts some interesting structural oddities along with the ghosts said to reside there. While the fraternity still occupied the house, there was the tradition that if a member willingly chose to live in a small room on the second floor nicknamed "the closet," that member would flunk out or move away from school. Another thing that is odd about the house are two particular features: an exterior door that doesn't lead inside the house and a window that isn't accessible from within the home. Staff members are quick to mention that these are merely the result of remodeling done to the interior of the house, and nothing paranormal is related to the changes.

Reflections

Today the Career Development Center serves the needs of students and alumni alike. For all the macabre stories that surround the building, the staff is cheery and always willing to help with a job application or assist with resume writing. They take comfort in the fact that even if the stories mention babies in the cellar or a ghostly girl roaming the halls, no human remains have ever been discovered on the property.

When I was nearing the time to graduate in 2007, I was constantly visiting the center to work on my Curriculum Vitae, an academic resume, for various university masters programs I was applying to. Although I knew of the paranormal stories about the CDC, nothing seemed out of the ordinary while I was there. I even attended a lecture in the basement that spring and, although the speaker bored me to death, I never once heard babies crying coming from within the walls.

Are the stories all bunk? It is hard to say, especially since finding some of the background of the house is difficult due to the university now owning the property. Some paranormal enthusiasts have brought up the idea that renovating a place where ghosts reside will stir up the activity. Did that happen here?

However, something to keep in mind is the subject matter of the stories. Illegal abortions are a hot topic that immediately evokes pity from many listeners. Using that emotional reaction in conjunction with knowledge of traditional conservative social values of abhorrence towards out-of-wedlock pregnancies creates a well-crafted tragic story. The tales of the "Good Doctor" in the CDC is strangely parallel to a real individual to live in the late nineteenth century: Dr. Henry Howard Holmes, whose real name was Herman Webster Mudgett. He was an American serial killer best known for his string of killings in Chicago around the 1893 World's Fair. Perhaps Holmes' activities were somehow superimposed through retellings of the "Good Doctor's" over time. Sometimes it seems that truth really can be stranger than fiction.

MEMORIAL MEMORIES

Rising above the treetops of Bloomington is a white pillar to Hoosier athletics known as "The Rock." With a capacity to seat 53,500 eager sport fans, a construction time of two years, and a cost of $4.56 million dollars, the Indiana University Memorial Stadium is one of the shining landmarks on this Midwestern college campus. Although the IU football team isn't what it once was, the stadium still remains a popular meeting place for alumni and current students during football weekends.

Rocky History

As mentioned in a different story for this book, Memorial Stadium is actually the second stadium to be built for the university's athletic use and the second to hold the name "Memorial Stadium." The first stadium was built in 1925 and sat on 10th Street overlooking much of the campus and Fess Avenue. Although at first the capacity to hold 20,000 cheering fans was magnificent, through the years the campus grew and the old Memorial Stadium grew obsolete. In 1958, ground was broken on 17th Street to complete a "new" Memorial Stadium. When it was completed October 8, 1960, it was an impressive new addition to the campus landscape. Through the years the stadium has had many renovations and additions so that it can continue serving the Hoosier football fan base.

A large limestone boulder was installed near the field in 2005; it was an accessory added when Terry Hoeppner became the head coach of the IU football team. The boulder now sits as a testament to Hoeppner's memory, for in 2007 he lost his battle with brain cancer. IU football fans may still be lamenting the loss of a beloved coach, but it's not the first time Memorial Stadium has had a touch with tragedy. Although Hoeppner's memory has forever been preserved through the limestone boulder, a memory from a decade's old mystery is preserved in the form of a ghost!

A Haunting Case

During the construction of the stadium, there was a horrible turn of events one February night — one that created a mystery in Bloomington that has remained unsolved for years. Fueled with speculation, no one knows how an unfortunate IU student named Michael Plume died. On February 15, 1960, Plume, an active member of the U.S. Air Force who was studying Russian at Indiana University, was found hanging from an eighteen-foot rope on the incomplete west side of Memorial Stadium — he was only nineteen-years-old.

Plume's death was full of questionable circumstances. His shoes were clean although he was found in the middle of a construction site. His feet were also found resting on the bed of a truck although his neck had been snapped. Officially, Plume's death was ruled a suicide by strangulation, however there are many members in the community who believe that Plume's death was really a homicide.

Rumors surrounded the case; some said that Plume died due to pressures of being a homosexual while others argued that he was murdered because of it. One classmate was reportedly overheard bragging about how he could kill someone and get away with it. The more extreme rumors claimed that it was espionage that did Plume in. Plume's father, William, never believed that his son committed suicide and petitioned local authorites to reopen the case in 1988, but his request was denied because the statute of limitations had expired.

It seems that Michael Plume never left the stadium...at least his spirit never did. Since the years of his unexplained death, there have been reports of a ghostly silhouette seen dangling from the beams on the west side of Memorial Stadium.

Melanie, a current member of the Indiana Ghost Trackers Bloomington chapter, was the one to notify me about the ghost. She had only heard the story as a rumor and was not aware of the true case behind Plume's death. She didn't even know that the ghost had a name! Since she was a teenager, however, there have been stories of how maintenance staff and even some unlucky football fans have run into Plume's shadowy specter hanging lifelessly from the rafters.

Reflections

This is one of those situations where a haunting could actually be taking place at this location. The recent history supports the ghostly phenomenon, which is usually something very hard to achieve at haunted places. It almost seems as if Michael Plume can't rest in peace, reaching out to the living in a desperate plea for his case to get another chance. Using such a shocking method, Plume is drawing attention to his situation, and that perhaps the truth has not yet been discovered.

THE McNUTT HATCHET MAN

Every year in late August, incoming freshmen are welcomed onto campus and settle into their new abodes that they'll call home for the next academic year. One popular dormitory freshmen find themselves in is McNutt, off of Fee Lane, in the northwest neighborhood of the campus.

A Bit of History

In the mid-twentieth century, Indiana University, under the direction of Herman B. Wells, felt that it needed to drastically expand its dormitory options. Since the end of World War II, the university has been constantly improving and expanding the buildings located on campus. In 1964, the Paul V. McNutt Residence Hall, "McNutt" for short, was completed. The residence hall is named after a former governor of Indiana who was known for tirelessly working in the Philippines in addition to his tenure as governor. A bronze bust of Paul McNutt stands in the main lobby of McNutt Residence Hall, adorned with ceremonial flags used during McNutt's time in the Philippines, as a reminder of the dormitory's namesake.

McNutt is actually made up of six five-story limestone buildings with two courtyards. Around the north courtyard sits the Bryan, Crone, and Bordner buildings; while the dorm buildings known as Dejoya, Bocobo, and Delgado sit around the south courtyard. Most dorm rooms are double occupancy; however there are also a few single or triple occupancy rooms available to students. The central building has undergone some remodeling, and starting in August 2009, will feature new classrooms, a new convenience store, and dining facilities.

The Hatchet Man

Although McNutt Dormitory is along the same street as many other campus residence halls such as Foster Dormitory and Briscoe Quadrangle, residents can still feel isolated from much of the campus. Perhaps this idea, coupled with a freshman's sudden lifestyle change to independence, makes McNutt the central part of our story. The legend goes that back in the late 1960s, a pair of co-eds was forced to stay on campus during Thanksgiving break for various reasons. Only a few days into the holiday break, the city of Bloomington issued a warning that a serial killer was on the loose and residents should stay indoors.

One roommate decided that she had enough of being cooped up and absolutely wanted to go have a fun night on the town, serial killer or not. So, ignoring the warnings and over her roommate's protests, she left her fear-stricken roommate behind and disappeared into a chilly November night. The co-ed left behind locked the door and tried not to worry about her friend.

About a half an hour passed when the co-ed staying in the dorm was startled to hear an eerie scratching sound emanating from behind her door. Terrified, the girl hid in her room's closet, convincing herself that it was the hatchet man out for her blood. The eerie sound continued for another half hour, gradually getting less intense and softer until they finally stopped. The girl, still too afraid to investigate, slept in her closet that night.

BAM! BAM! BAM!

The girl was woken by a hard pounding on her door the next morning. Sunlight filtered through the blinds as she timidly crossed the room. In a trembling voice, the girl asked, "Who's there?" The reply soothed her terrified soul — it was the police. She flung the door open to find a bloody scene in the hallway. A black body bag sat off to the side and policemen in uniforms were marking blood pools that led from the dorm room's door to the building's front door. A police photographer was busily taking photos of the hallway.

In horror, the co-ed listened to her close encounter with the Hatchet Man. He had reportedly been seen prowling around Fee Lane that night; she was lucky that she had been safe in her room, but one co-ed wasn't so fortunate — her roommate. From what the police could make of the situation, the unlucky girl had forgotten something in her room and had turned around to go back to the dormitory to fetch it. If she hadn't had done this, she may have survived to see another day, but instead the poor girl ran into the Hatchet Man! He buried a hatchet into the back of her skull and left her for dead in front of McNutt. She didn't die immediately; she managed to slowly crawl into the dormitory and even made it to her room's door! Finding it locked, she scratched in hopes of getting the attention of her roommate, but to no avail. The unlucky girl perished before her door due to massive blood loss.

Immediately after hearing the story, the surviving roommate was asked to identify the victim's body. Before the girl could object, the black body bag was unzipped, revealing the wide-eyed corpse, mangled from fright, her face twisted in agony!

As a Matter of Fact...

This story sounds like something straight out of the movies: gory, tragic, and really makes you think twice before entering into the unforgiving night. Thankfully, this terror tale is just that...*a tale*. It's probably one of the most common urban legends ever recorded. The "Roommate's Death," as it has been commonly called, has existed around college campuses since the early 1960s. There are many variations to this legend, even on IU's campus. The decades, order of events, and even the method of killing differ in each account.

Although this is a common urban legend, there are those who see a glimmer of truth between the lines. It has been speculated that the origin of this story was the Speck Murders that took place in Chicago on July 14, 1966. Richard Speck snuck into the student nurse's dormitory for South Chicago Community Hospital around 11 p.m. on July 13th. Back then the dormitory was a renovated old home, not the large dormitory commonly thought of on large university campuses. He meticulously bound and killed the eight student nurses who lived in the dormitory by either stabbing them to death or strangling them one-by-one. There was only one survivor — Corazon Amurao had managed to hide under a bed and avoid Speck's murderous rampage. Speck was convicted of his crime and sentenced to the death penalty, which was later changed to life in prison. He died in prison in 1991 at the age of forty-nine.

Reflections

The tale of the "McNutt Hatchet Man" is well-known within the campus community and is commonly told during the first week of school for freshmen. Retelling stories about the campus — creepy or not — seems to be a way students learn about each other. The "McNutt Hatchet Man" story has its place in IU lore, along with the Read Dormitory ghosts and the "Good Doctor" of the Career Development Center. Variations of this urban legend exist on many other major universities and colleges around the United States, making it as well-known as the Vanishing Hitch-hiker tale. Although the story may have been inspired by a true event, as many of them are, students can be assured that the story is only an urban legend.

OWEN HALL'S MISSING PARTS

Situated among the Old Crescent buildings on campus is historic Owen Hall. The squat brick building and its sister Wylie Hall are the oldest buildings on campus to survive until today. Owen and Wylie Halls are the only buildings on the entire campus that have brick exteriors instead of Indiana limestone, so they resemble buildings on Purdue University's campus more than the department buildings of Indiana University. Completed in 1885, Owen Hall first housed the Department of Natural Sciences and the University museum. Through the years it has been the location of different departments, from the Chancellor's offices to the current School of Continuing Education. Because of the original use of the building for the school of Natural Sciences, over the years many grizzly stories have crept into the campus body regarding cadavers and lost limbs.

Owen Hall sits in the middle of the "Old Crescent" area of campus — and may be home to a ghost or two. *Illustration by Liz Fuller.*

The Legends

The Nurse with the Cadaver Arm

The first legend involves nursing students from the mid-twentieth century. Circulating around campus, especially among medical students, is the legend of the nursing student and the cadaver arm. As the legend goes, a girl was attending Indiana University's nursing program, but was not well liked in her class. Her peers thought she was a bit too pretentious and spoiled, and that she acted like they were all inferior students compared to her academic record. In an attempt to adjust the girl's attitude, a male nursing student stole into Owen Hall's cadaver lab and sliced off an arm of the nearest body he found. With his roommate and a few other students as his accomplices, the student tied the cadaver arm to the overhead light's pull string. The group, smug with their joke, snuck outside the dormitory and hid beneath the window of the girl's dorm room to await her return home from work later that night.

The nursing student returned home tired after a long shift at work and entered her room, completely unaware of the plot against her. The group of students listened to her enter the room and switch on the light, but instead of the blood-curdling scream expected out of her silence fell over the room. Puzzled, the group of students made their way back into the dorm to check on their target. They snuck down the hallway and peered into the room since the door was ajar, where they noticed that the cadaver arm was no longer hanging by the pull cord! The group moved into the dorm room to further investigate and were greeted with the horrifying sight of the nursing student gnawing on the arm rocking back and forth with her eyes glossy but wide open. The girl's hair had been shocked to white by the discovery of the bloody stump hanging in her room. The group had not improved the girl's mind-set...instead they had managed to drive her insane.

Ghostly Limbs

The second story about Owen Hall regards the many years it housed donated cadavers for student dissections. The building is said to be rigged with a dumb-waiter that was used to hoist bodies to the upper floors for classes. Many times, according to legend, limbs would get stuck or tear off as the bodies were sent up the small shaft, never to be retrieved after falling down to the bottom. Stories have circulated in hushed voices about the ghosts of the donated cadavers haunting the hall. There have also been reports of cold spots being felt around the building as well as objects moving around the rooms of their own accord. Objects have gone missing as well, only to reappear sometime after they were no longer needed.

Reflections

These stories are nothing more than campus lore with no facts to really back them up. In the case of the cadaver's arm, it is a common urban legend that has been adapted into the university's setting; it has been circulating since the 1920s, told to "shock and awe" its audience for entertainment purposes. There are many versions of the legend as well, sometimes replacing the arm with a hand that is placed in a nursing student's bed. The final results are similar too, with the student's hair turning white from shock and her dining on the dismembered limb. Although many versions of the urban legend include bloody dismembered limbs as the main subject of the story, dissected limbs for academic study are rarely bloody. This is due to the blood being drained from the donated cadavers and replaced with formaldehyde before being presented to a university for learning purposes.

Owen Hall does not appear to be haunted, regardless of its grizzly past. That story too is just a popular legend that was passed by word of mouth in the earlier part of the twentieth century. Every day people work in the offices in Owen Hall and although it looks creepy at night, employees come back the next day unharmed. Many older buildings are supposed to be haunted since they are, well, old. It gives the building character as well as a scapegoat whenever something a little odd or unfortunate occurs in the area. In the end, the stories are entertaining and a fun way of preserving the history of the building.

LA CASA LADY

With its bright gray Indiana limestone exterior and red-tiled roof, Indiana University's Latino Culture Center welcomes everyone in the IU community into its friendly offices. Led by active and enthusiastic staff members, "La Casa" (Spanish for "the house") has been a welcoming environment for social programs and student groups focusing on Latino and Latina culture to flourish on campus. One of the integral parts of this home's community, though, isn't what every cultural center could brag to have — a ghostly woman that calls La Casa her eternal home. I call the spirit "La Casa Lady."

La Historia

Not much is known about the current building's history before the university purchased it in 1976 other than it was a private residence. The Office of Latino Affairs was created in January of 1973 to service the growing academic, social, and cultural needs of the Latino populations on the Indiana University Bloomington campus. Later that year, the donation of a house to serve as the first Latino Cultural Center was announced to great acclaim, with the Latino Cultural Center located at 410 South Park Avenue, on the south side of campus off of East Atwater Avenue. Students and staff at the Office of Latino Affairs named their new cultural center "La Casa."

La Casa resided at that address for over three years before it moved to its present location at 715 East Seventh Street, just northwest of the Indiana Memorial Union. The new home was larger than the previous accommodations at 1,200 square feet and, with the additional room, the Chicano-Riqueno Studies Research Library was created. La Casa has been on East Seventh Street for over thirty years.

El Fantasma

When the students and staff moved the La Casa Center into their new location, they didn't expect to already have a spectral housemate! Through the years they have reported numerous forms of paranormal activity, with one of the more frequent occurrences being the sound of the office typewriter typing away. However, when investigated, no one is found at the old, unplugged, and covered typewriter!

The ghost of the La Casa Latino Cultural Center is one of the most well-known ghosts on campus. *Illustration by Kat Klockow.*

Besides the unexplainable sounds being made by the old type-writer, the figure of a woman has been seen multiple times in various situations. The La Casa Lady is known to like her house full of light... when staff members close up the cultural center at the end of a long day, they can see a silhouette of a female going around and turning the lights back on. After checking to make sure no one has been left in the house, staffers can only assume it was the La Casa Lady.

Other times, when the staff and students are closing up for the night, they hear the unmistakable sounds of someone running either up and down the stairwell or up and down the second floor hallway. Again the staff member would check to make sure that no stray student was being locked up in the house, but no one physically could be found.

The second floor seems to be the La Casa Lady's favorite area of the home. Staff members have seen her dark silhouette silently walking down the second floor corridor as they work during the day. She also seems to like staring out the upstairs windows, as passersby have reported seeing a transparent woman clad in white. After being discovered, though, she fades away, back into the inky darkness.

Reflections

The ghostly La Casa Lady has become part of La Casa Cultural Center's history and the staff seems to have taken pride in their home's ghost. While some members of the staff tend to be a bit nervous about potentially meeting La Casa's resident ghost, most of the community appear enthusiastic to have had their own personal experiences with her. In this case, the students and staff of La Casa have largely embraced their house ghost, seeing her as an esteemed member of their community — and La Casa Lady seems to be as equally smitten with her new family as they are with her.

SPECTRALS AT THE
KELLEY SCHOOL OF BUSINESS

Indiana University is home to one of the best business schools in America, the nationally ranked Kelley School of Business. Located on the corners of Fee Lane and 10th Street in the northeast neighborhood of the campus, it sits across the Arboretum. Internationally recognized students from the United States and abroad converge at the school every year, making campus life even more diverse and exciting. With all the activity around the school, maybe it stands to reason that they have attracted a ghost or two.

Prestigious History

The school was originally established in 1829 as the School of Commerce and Finance, making it one of the oldest continuous departments at Indiana University. In 1932, the school's name changed to the School of Business Administration, only to be shortened in 1938 to the School of Business. The school kept that name until 1997, when E. W. Kelley gave a gift of $23 million dollars to the business school. The university renamed it the Kelley School of Business in his honor. The school has both undergraduate and graduate programs, the latter of the two was established in 1961. Undergraduates interested in the school of business can enroll in a myriad of workshops and clubs to prepare themselves for graduate work.

The school has moved around the Indiana University campus as the enrolled student body has grown. From 1923 to 1940, it was located in Rawles Hall in the southwest side of campus near the Old Crescent. In 1940, it moved to Woodburn Hall where the department stayed until its move in 1966 to its present building. The building that the Kelley School of Business now occupies was completed in 1966 and actually is two buildings joined together by a pedestrian footbridge suspended over Fee Lane.

Haunted Hallways

For all the achievements the Kelley School of Business brings to the university, there is an air of mystery within its halls. Staff members have reported the sounds of disembodied footsteps throughout the halls, as well as doors opening and closing without aid long after the traditional school hours have passed. Upon inspection of the origin of the sounds, no explanation can be found...it is as if spectral students are walking the halls of the school building.

An Indiana University security officer has reported some unusual happenings occurring during the graveyard watch of the Kelley School of Business buildings. According to the officer, he followed the sound of suspicious footsteps into a second floor lecture hall. Once in the hall, the officer claimed to have witnessed one of the many folding lecture hall seats slowly being pushed down by invisible hands followed by the distinct sound of someone sitting in the seat. Chilled at what he saw, he left the room quickly.

On another account, an officer was alarmed while patrolling the building when he heard what was described to be a shrill squeal coming from a stairwell at 4 a.m. After searching the area extensively, the officer found no evidence of the perpetrator. For the rest of the night, he wondered what it was that he had heard.

Reflections

Who haunts the Kelley School of Business?

In the case of the lecture hall, it seems to be a spirit that is as dedicated to their studies in death as they were in life. It could very well be not an interactive spirit, but rather a residual one, practicing its daily ritual of arriving to class. Like many other schools and departments around the campus, the business school has its share of stresses and frustrations, and perhaps these emotions have been imprinted into the limestone building.

In the case of the squeal coming from the staircase, perhaps its origin can be found in the natural world, not the paranormal one. It could have been a squeaking door or an unauthorized student or two walking the halls of the building after hours. The possibilities are endless. Noises can take a more sinister or ghostly manner when being perceived by people alone in a large, dark building at night. Personally I have seen it on ghost hunts or investigations where members become convinced that everything around them is spooky and that ghosts are literally everywhere.

Without further investigation or data, the reports coming out of the Kelley School of Business are just stories...told and circulated around campus to keep a student's interest while in lectures. Stories such as these help to give flavor to the academic environment and personality to the places where students spend a good portion of their time studying. These stories, and the ghosts in them, are harmless.

VARIOUS IU LEGENDS

Over the course of Indiana University's long history, it has managed to accumulate many legends. Some are about traditions that are still practiced today on campus while others are just old amusing tales circulated around the student body. However, these tales are essential to the culture at IU, and few students graduate without learning about them...

The Sinking of Main Library

One of the most popular and often asked about legends to exist on campus is the legend of the main library sinking steadily into the earth. As the legend goes, the original architect of the building neglected to accommodate the weight of all the hundreds of millions of books held within the stacks of the main library. This resulted with unaccounted weight now forcing the entire building to sink an inch a year.

It turns out that this is a very common urban legend, one that seems to be present on many college campuses across the United States and perhaps beyond. The main library, renamed the Herman B. Wells Library in 2005, is a gigantic double tower structure built in 1969. Within its Indiana Limestone walls sit 4.6 million books, magazines, newspapers, and films. The question has come up so often that from time-to-time an explanation of how it is impossible for the library to sink into the earth appears in alumni newsletters and on the main library site. Why isn't the library sinking? Two reasons: the weight of the books was in fact accounted for when the blue prints were drafted and the campus sits on a bed of limestone. Nothing will ever sink into the earth around campus because of this prehistoric rock bed.

Mr. Wells Waves

On October 21, 2000, a statue was dedicated in the Old Crescent area of campus to a beloved and much admired past leader, university president, and chancellor of Indiana University, Herman B. Wells. He is one of the key individuals who helped make Indiana University what it is today. The statue is a life-sized sculpture cast in bronze that sits on a bench surrounded by roses across from the

Rose Well House. His statue is a popular place to take pictures while visiting the campus — and it's said to *come alive* in the wee hours of the morning.

No one has ever caught this event on tape, but rumor has it that his statue will wave at passing students...or sometimes get up and walk around of its own accord! However, it is hard to take this legend for anything more than hearsay since the statue sits in the thruway between the active Kirkwood Avenue district and many of the student dormitories. Since many of the restaurants and bars close within the "witching hours" (2 to 3 a.m.), one has to only guess what is causing the sight of the moving Wells Statue.

The Rose Well House

If at the stroke of midnight a female student is kissing her honey, she will become a full fledged co-ed at Indiana University — that's the legend anyway. The Rose Well House in the Old Crescent area of campus has been a popular place to kiss your sweetheart from nearly the day it was erected in 1908. Sometimes just referred to as the "Well House," the structure is built over the first water cistern constructed on campus and its architecture is meant to resemble the shape of a Beta Theta Pi Fraternity pin.

This legend originated within years of the Well House being constructed, when there were strict curfews at the dormitories and the male and female students stayed in separate buildings made out of Victorian decorum. The dorm mothers would lock the doors to their resident halls, so kissing a sweetheart at midnight was a blatant disregard of the campus rules — and thus participants would gain prestige from this rebellious act.

As time progressed, however, it was only natural for the story to change to suit the needs of the current student class. Presently female students are far more common on college campuses across the United States and, in the case of Indiana University, they actually make up the majority of students. The story has morphed to fit these new needs: if any student kisses their sweetheart at the Rose Well House through the twelve strokes of midnight on Valentine's Day, the couple's love for each other will be eternal. Couples have been known to line up around the small structure to kiss on Valentine's Day starting early in the evening for the chance to kiss in the small edifice at midnight.

It should be noted that there is some confusion whether the good luck will happen in the presence of the Rose Well House or Beck Chapel. Traditionally, it is the Rose Well House that the custom

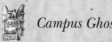

The Rose Well Pump House is the site for many classic folklores around Indiana University. *Illustration by Liz Fuller.*

originated with, but it's also possible to see groups of students on Valentine's Day at either campus landmark waiting for the stroke of midnight. Both locations seem to bring about the same amount of luck and love for those who are willing to participate in this century-old campus tradition.

Bell Tolls & Fish Fly

Another legend at IU focuses on the Student Building on graduation day. The only building on campus to have a bell tower is the Student Building located in the Old Crescent area of campus. Currently the building houses the Anthropology and Geography department offices, labs, and classrooms. As the old campus legend goes, if a virgin graduates from the university, the bells will toll widely on graduation day. This story never made any sense to me as a student...because the bells DO toll on graduation day as a form of festivity and congratulations to the graduates.

There is another version of the "graduating virgin" legend on campus: if a virgin graduates from the university, the fish in the Showalter Fountain located in the middle of the Fine Arts Plaza will come to life and jump high in the air. A variant of this legend is that the Showalter Venus will be born on that day, stemming from the subject of the fountain — the birth of Venus.

Legends about graduation day virgins don't just exist on IU's campus; many universities have their own variations. For example, at the University of Cincinnati, the two stone lions on campus are supposed to roar when virgins graduate from the university. These stories are meant to be amusing bits of fiction, but interestingly enough, I heard this story while at freshmen orientation in 2002!

1998

One of the more frightening legends was to take place over a decade ago at Indiana University. It was rumored that on a talk show late in the summer before the fall semester started, a physic predicted that Indiana University was to be the site of a chain of horrible murders. The murders were to take place in a dormitory that was in the shape of an "X" or "V," and it was going to happen on Halloween by a culprit dressed up as Little-bo Peep. The day arrived and members of the student body held their breath for the ill-fated turn of events, but fortunately the prediction never came to pass.

This is another example of an urban legend that has circulated around from university to university for quite a number of years. Sometimes the added detail of a "university that starts with an "M" or "W" has been cited in the story in addition to the description of the building's form, which caused much grief at the University of Minnesota, University of Michigan, and the University of Wisconsin back then. Many universities use the "X" or "V" form for a dormitory's construction, so the story can be changed easily to fit the local university culture.

Jordan Boating

The following legend is said to have taken place in the 1990s and is retold every spring when the "mighty" Jordan River (formerly Spanker's Branch) overflows its banks and grows three times as large. According to the legend, a student named River brought his own canoe or kayak to maneuver through the river, but tipped over and was washed into the sewer system under the campus!

Shockingly, this story is partly true. Although a student named River and his canoe may never have existed, a twenty-year-old male student was swept into the underground sewer system in 1993. This drenched and bewildered male student was sent downstream from Sixth and Indiana avenues, under the city streets, and was eventually rescued by the Bloomington City Police Department when he popped out of the other side of the system near Walnut and First streets. The student had the ride of his life, being sucked three-quarters of a mile through water passageway.

Those Sneakers

The final legend can be seen dotted around the campus and streets surrounding the university: sneakers dangling helplessly from power lines. Throwing these old sneakers up onto the power lines is only a ritual, but why they are thrown up there has become campus legend. According to sources, there are three main reasons why the sneakers end up there: to signal that the owner of those sneakers is no longer a virgin, to announce that they have been invited to join a fraternity or sorority, and finally to announce their graduation. In all three situations, those participating in throwing shoes up into the power lines see it as an act of celebration.

Reflections

These are just a handful of campus legends that have been celebrated or talked about through the years by the student body. Some legends or rituals can be found at other universities such as "the graduating virgins" paranormal events while others like those that take place in the Rose Well House are truly unique to Indiana University Bloomington's campus. Whether they are gruesome, humorous, or romantic, special legends are what give flavor to a university's culture.

2

BLOOMINGTON
& BEYOND

AFTER-HOURS TERRORS

BLOOMINGTON'S HAUNTED SCHOOLS

Usually when we think of a school we think of a safe place where our children learn and play in a positive environment. Although this is generally the case, some schools have a special dash of personality of their own and, in the case of three schools in the City of Bloomington... hauntingly so. (*Author's Note: Their names of the schools are identified only by a letter of the alphabet to protect their integrity as institutions of education.)

School Q

Caring for students' educational needs for many years, School Q is a positive environment for the local children to learn and grow. It has a caring staff of teachers and administrators who keep the school running and provide assistance to the students and their parents. At night, however, when most have gone home, two shadowy phantoms claim the school as their own....

Legend has it that the first ghost is that of an old janitor who was traumatically killed in one of the closets of the school by a gang of older students. A few decades ago the school accommodated both elementary and middle school students. It was during this time that the janitor was allegedly killed. It's unknown why he would have been killed and no records have ever indicated that such an act was committed on the property. Nonetheless, his spirit has been seen roaming around the halls wearing nothing but black by fellow janitorial staff at night. When approached, the shadowy ghost disappears.

The second story involves the untimely death of a young student on the premises. As the story goes, in the 1970s a young male student was participating in a student play and had to get up onto the catwalk above the stage. The young boy lost his balance and plummeted to the floor of the auditorium; he was killed instantly. From then on, staff, students, and visitors to the school's auditorium have seen a black figure running across the catwalks. The ghost has been described as wearing a black cloak or cape.

Although both of these stories are frightening, no evidence has ever been found that they are true. The legends just seem to be amusing bits of folklore to give macabre personality to the school.

School X

Another school in Bloomington with an eerie atmosphere is School X. Like School Q, during the day, when students and faculty are around, the overall environment is positive. However, when night falls, those who are there late have found that some very spooky things take place.

According to local legend, there is a male ghost that appears as a shadowy figure and lurks in the halls, closets, and bathrooms on the east side of the building. Female staff members seem to be the common target of this entity.

According to a staff member I'll call "Jessica," female staff who have used the faculty restrooms have had a few scares. In one incident, a faculty member was locked inside one of the bathroom stalls. While she struggled to open the stall door, she noticed that water was beginning to flood out of the drain located just outside the stall. With one great push, she managed to open the door; she then ran out of the bathroom and reported the drain's water problem to maintenance. Apparently there have been many reported problems with this certain drain pipe. Through the years, people have reported it randomly flooding the bathroom. When maintenance staff open up the sealed drain and peek inside, they find it is mysteriously stuffed with toilet paper and paper towels. Jessica doesn't know what to make of that, as she doesn't think any of the faculty would do such a thing on purpose.

Other unexplainable phenomena to be reported in the women's faculty restroom have been apparitions in mirrors, the faucets turning on and off on their own, and lights ominously flickering. Maintenance has checked repeatedly to make sure the lights and faucets are in working order, and they always seem to check out okay. As for the apparitions in the mirrors, that's a whole different ball game.

There is a closet nestled between a set of male and female restrooms elsewhere in the school that has reportedly sent chills up people's spines when they walk by. The closet seems to give off uneasy feelings of terror, panic, or dread to people passing by the area. I even found myself avoiding this particular closet on the way to use the restroom the first time I visited the site, at the time being completely unaware of the terrors people have experienced in that area. Cold spots, sounds of footsteps, and a shadowy apparition have been seen walking down a corridor in the building that links the restrooms and janitor's closet.

The Investigation

Indiana Ghost Trackers Bloomington has investigated the school twice in recent years, in January 2008 and January 2009, on the request of one of the faculty members. It was the January 2009 meeting that I was present at, although I did not "ghost hunt" with the group afterwards.

In the most recent visit, IGT-Bloomington had quite an exciting night. Like usual, the group of investigators split into smaller groups. One group, led by Melanie, had some unexplained occurrences in one room of the building, including sudden headaches or the feeling of heavy-headedness. They also experienced a cold spot after a team member, Rob, had asked a question and recorded a strange message that sounded similar to walkie-talkie interference. No explanation could be found for this noise. Finally, while still in this room, team members were struck with sudden yet unexplainable "bad" or "negative" emotions. Once team members left the room, however, those emotions quickly disappeared.

The southern corridor in the school building has a reputation for supernatural occurrences and has been the focus of many unexplained incidents, which the paranormal team was able to support. While gathering data in the corridor, Melanie's team was asking questions to any entity that happened to be in the area. In response to one of these questions, there was an ear-piercing screech! The occurrence could be attributed to coincidence and interference with the walkie-talkie system, but it was an odd coincidence nonetheless. Sometime later a guest with the team suddenly freaked out, claiming that they saw someone standing near the storage room doors. Upon exploring the area, though, no one was found to be there but the team members. Was the guest having a terrifying personal experience or was it something else? Sometimes it is a hard call to make.

Another small group led by IGT-Bloomington member Linda had some remarkable experiences of their own while traversing a particular room in the school. As the group entered the staff lounge to gather data, they were welcomed by a chair moving by itself in front of them! Later, as the group sat together, a team member noticed a strange shadow near the hall door. The group watched in amazement as the shadow started to slide under the hall door into the room with them. The group kept their calm...snapping pictures and recording as much information as they could before exiting the room.

School K

Last but not least is School K, which seems to have a habit of scaring the janitorial staff. School K has a long history in the area, with many locations and additions through the years to its building. As time has progressed, however, it seems to have picked up a mysterious ghost that has been seen walking the halls after the children have left the premises.

This mysterious ghost is a female — staff have witnessed "her" numerous times walking down the main hallways of the school after traditional school hours have ceased. She has been described as being a fairly young woman, maybe in her 20s, and she's always seen wearing a one-piece dress flowing down to her knees. She appears suddenly in the hallway and, as she walks away from the witness down the hall, she gradually fades away, leaving the poor witness in utter disbelief.

Reflections

Questions abound when it comes to haunted schools. Who haunts these locations and why? What kind of connection could a spirit have that keeps the need to visit the schools so intense? In the case of schools K and Q, the stories really just seem to be local legends, maybe spread around the student body to give a spooky history to the school. In School X, though, something definitely intelligent roams the halls at night and scares the faculty during the day. No deaths have ever been reported at any of the schools, so we end up with a quandary. If no one has died there, what is *it* in those halls?

AZALIA BRIDGE

Heinous Stories and Gory Legends

Just outside of Seymour, Indiana, in Bartholomew County is the small town of Azalia. Named for the flower that grows throughout the area, Azalia was founded in 1831 along the shore of Sand Creek. Usually a quiet town, Azalia is known for one particularly paranormal bridge that draws in curiosity seekers and paranormal enthusiasts every full moon. Why? Because a spectral group of ghosts is said to haunt the bridge and the creek around it!

The Woman on the Riverbank

The first story that involves Azalia Bridge is said to have happened in the earlier days of Azalia's history. Back then, family farms dotted the landscape miles apart. One such farm was owned by an older gentleman and was located near where the current Azalia Bridge is located now. One day, the old farmer left for an extended period of time and, when he returned, he had a new young bride by his side. The marriage seemed to be a happy one for a while...until the day the old farmer found his wife in the arms of a younger man. One evening the farmer happened to find the couple locked in an embrace on the banks of Sand Creek. Instantly, the farmer flew into a rage, and took out his rusty farming knife and charged at the couple. Perhaps he meant to assault the young man, but instead he attacked his wife, slitting her throat so deeply that it completely decapitated her. The young man, now the focus of the farmer's anger, took out his pistol and aimed. When the farmer charged, he shot one round that struck the farmer square in the forehead, killing him instantly.

Rumor has it now that the horrendous apparition of the tragic young woman has been seen wandering the riverbank by motorists passing over Azalia Bridge. Some say that the murders of her and her husband were the first case of double homicide reported in Azalia. According to local legend, it is seen as a death omen upon those who see the headless form of the young woman: If you see her apparition carrying her head in the river, you'll be fine...but if you catch a glimpse of her without her head entirely, you will die within the year!

The decapitated woman isn't the only specter said to haunt the area around the bridge. Joining her is a tragic young couple who were killed as they crossed the bridge one night on their way to a dance. On some nights, motorists have heard the spine-chilling screams of the young couple as they have crossed the bridge. Other motorists have said they have seen shadow figures walking the banks of the river towards the bridge, but as they reach the bridge, they simply fade into the air.

The Vanishing Pair

Azalia Bridge has become the focal point of a popular urban legend in the countryside. As the story goes, a young teenage couple has been

The ghost stories about Azalia Bridge are probably some of the best known legends in Southern Indiana. *Illustration by Kat Klockow.*

seen trying to flag down motorists as they approach Azalia Bridge late at night. It is said that numerous times a motorist has picked up the young couple who ask to be driven to a certain address in town. Once they arrive at the address, the driver turns around to say goodbye to the young couple only to be met with an eerily empty backseat. Confused, the driver goes up and rings the doorbell of the home. After meeting an older gentleman who opens the door, the driver is shocked to discover that the couple had in fact passed away several years earlier in a horrible car accident. The couple, rushing home to make the girl's curfew, lost control of the car and ran off of Azalia Bridge right in the location where the driver picked them up. The older gentleman also notes that every year at this time — the anniversary of the couple's car accident — he always opens the door to meet some bewildered motorist who swears that they had just picked up the young couple.

This chilling tale is just a localization of the common urban legend of the Vanishing Hitchhiker. Although a great ghost story that includes an interesting twist to the plot, the story is surprisingly not restricted to twenty-first century roads and highways. Stories about vanishing carriage passengers dot colonial era folk tales while Hawaiian narratives tell about the Volcano Goddess Pele hitching rides from islanders. There are also just as many variations to the story as there are towns where it takes place in. Some variations say that the vanishing passenger leaves an article of clothing, sometimes a damp or cold spot in the back seat, or even adjusts the age and sex of the hitchhiker in question. In this variation, we have a pair of hitchhikers who have been localized by dying at the foot of Azalia Bridge.

Reflections

These stories are chilling whether they are fact or fiction, but there are some details to consider when listening to any ghost story or urban legend: What is the land like? Does history support these claims, and how long have these stories been around? While asking locals about the stories surrounding the bridge, I came to find out that it is a fairly busy intersection. Accidents do happen at the bridge, which may explain why the Vanishing Hitchhiker story was adapted so easily here. I also found out that the environment around the bridge just seems to beg for a ghost story to happen. Many times during the year Sand Creek creates a wonderful wall of fog, making the bridge look as if it has come right out of a horror movie. Perhaps these stories have fulfilled a craving to have a ghost story occur in the backyards of so many residents. Ghost stories add a bit of pizzazz and mystery to an otherwise ordinary location, such as Azalia Bridge.

SHADOW PEOPLE AT ROSE HiLL CEMETERY

One of the largest — if not *the* largest — cemetery in Bloomington is Rose Hill Cemetery. The expanse of the cemetery borders 4th Street, 3rd Street, West Kirkwood Avenue, Maple Street, and South Adams Street, just west of Bloomington Square. Nestled amongst a residential community, Rose Hill remains a popular place for both residents of Bloomington and students of Indiana University to take afternoon strolls through the aging headstones. However, when nighttime encompasses the sleepy cemetery in its inky darkness, the spirits of Bloomington's past walk along the graves…. If you're lucky, you may run into one of them!

Mysterious History

There are no burial records for Rose Hill Cemetery before October 6, 1897. The oldest portion of the cemetery is located at the southeast corner of the cemetery, bordered by Maple and 3rd Streets. It is estimated that this part of the cemetery was started between the years 1818 and 1820, when Indiana University and the city of Bloomington were just starting to grow. This particular location was chosen for being "out in the country, about a mile west of town," according to the county commissioners of that time. Since then, the city has grown around the old cemetery.

Rose Hill is not the original name of the cemetery. For a long time it was just labeled the "graveyard." In order for the local workmen and visitors to find the graveyard easily, the initials "G.Y." were carved into the trunk of a large Oak Tree located at the entrance (now long gone). Over time the name was changed to "City Cemetery," a more eloquent name to describe the place for Bloomington's dead. The name was changed once again in 1892 when the Ladies Cemetery Association, a local civic committee, took over its management. They changed and improved much of the landscape within the grounds of the cemetery in addition to granting it the romantic name "Rose Hill Cemetery." In fact, the entrance gate off of 4th Street is engraved with "Rose Hill Cemetery 1892" and has a carving of a rose in the limestone sign.

In 1893, a fountain was added to the center of the cemetery, also known as the Evergreen Arbor. The Evergreen Arbor is the title given to a circular arrangement of pine trees in the cemetery that still stand today. The fountain has since been moved to Bryan Park in Bloomington, but the circular

Rose Hill Cemetery is wonderful place to discover Bloomington's historic past.

stand of trees now play witness to a large round-about and planter full of seasonal flowers. It is because of these women that we are able to walk along neat cemetery paths and rest on benches around the cemetery and enjoy the scenery of southern Indiana in tranquility.

Ghostly Tales

The Evergreen Arbor seems to play host to a number of supernatural stories in Bloomington. According to locals, this area of the cemetery is regarded to be the most paranormally active. Around the band of pine trees, witnesses walking in the cemetery around dusk have seen shadow people dart along the trees as if they are watching the visitor's every move. Shadowy figures have also been caught seen walking along the tombstones wearing period clothing of the 1800s...only to vanish when perceived by onlookers. Cold spots have also been reported in the cemetery, as well as disembodied voices heard calling across the graveyard or whispering into the ears of bewildered visitors. Perhaps the shadows are figures from Bloomington and Indiana University's past? With such significant figures as musician Hoagy Carmichael (1899-1981), Indiana University Greek professor Reverend Elisha Ballantine (1809-1886), the namesake of Ballentine Hall, Indiana University mathematics professor Daniel Kirkwood (1814-1895), the namesake of Kirkwood Avenue and Kirkwood Hall, and past Indiana Governor Paris C. Dunning (1806-1884) buried in Rose Hill's hallowed ground, they may be visiting the living to see what their efforts have accomplished.

The Investigation

According to the stories, no one has ever been harmed by the shadow people that roam the old section of Rose Hill Cemetery; visitors are merely startled by the sight of featureless shadow forms walking along the headstones. I asked the local paranormal investigative team Indiana Ghost Trackers Bloomington about their experiences at the cemetery.

"When we don't have a place to hunt, we go there," says Lisa Bradley, director of IGT Bloomington's chapter, "but we don't find much there."

The group has made it an ongoing investigation site due to proximity and easy access. It is also a great place for new members of the team to practice using their equipment and get accustomed to the "ghost hunting" process. The team believes that many of the stories have been concocted by students or young residents to the area in an effort to scare each other. It isn't uncommon to find a group of teenagers or college students roaming around the cemetery in the middle of the night looking for a good scare, something that the city's Parks and Recreation Department frowns upon. Many times, after psyching themselves out, the students will go running out of the cemetery screaming — certain

One of Bloomington's most famous people, Hogey Carmichael, is buried here, along with his family. *Photo by Kat Klockow.*

that they had seen something paranormal, even if it really was quite explainable. Around Halloween there is a surge in visitors looking for ghosts around the cemetery.

Reflections

Whether there are shadow people lurking along the century-old headstones or not, Rose Hill is an impressive turn-of-the-century cemetery. Neatly landscaped and still holding its timelessly tranquil atmosphere, Rose Hill is an excellent place to get to know Bloomington's history. While there, I admired the various intricately-carved headstones for each family; from tree stumps carved from Indiana limestone to neatly carved veiled urns made of marble, Rose Hill Cemetery is as much of a treat to the eyes as its ghosts are to paranormal enthusiasts! Take a walk through timeless Rose Hill Cemetery — who knows, you may find yourself face-to-face with a member of Bloomington's historic past.

Planted in 1892 by the Ladies Cemetery Association, these evergreens are some of the oldest trees in the cemetery.

THE TUNNELTON LIGHTS

Located thirty-seven miles south of Bloomington in Lawrence County is the town of Tunnelton, Indiana. Most people commuting between Indianapolis and Louisville, Kentucky, will drive by the signs directing them to the city without much thought about what makes this town special. However, some paranormal enthusiasts know very well what is located in the outskirts of the city — the Tunnelton Tunnel. The tunnel boasts being one of the longest continuous train tunnels in the United States, at an astounding 1,750 feet long. With great popularity comes some local legends and, of course, some of those legends are about ghosts....

Dark History

Today the CSX Railway Company owns and operates the train tracks that lead through the Tunnelton Tunnel, but back in 1857 the railroad was built for the Ohio and Mississippi Railway. In 1898, the railway company commissioned local workers to line the earthen tunnel with brick since debris falling onto the tracks was a serious problem. One of the most prominent characteristics of the train tunnel is its "dead man's niches," which are closet-sized gaps in the walls of the tunnel every few feet. The purpose of these niches was to provide shelter for workers in the tunnel should a train pass through while they worked. One of the problems for tunnels of that time period was balancing airflow: if a train was to pass through and a man not make it into a niche, he would be sucked under the heavy iron train and ground into the earth. It is a very grizzly way to die, but a very real possibility for workers on the track.

Ghostly Legends

Dixon the Watchman

The first legend involving the tunnel is set over a hundred years ago when train travel was much more prevalent and most carved out tunnels were still earthen. According to the story, Dixon was the day watchman in charge of minding the train tracks by keeping them free of fallen debris. Eventually the train company that owned the line commissioned to have a layer of bricks cover the bare earth and keep the frequency of falling debris to a minimum. This required a troop of bricklayers to work in the tunnel during the day. Bricklayers during that time period were the sort of men who were of unsavory character, and most people trying to keep out of trouble would keep out of their way.

One day, while the bricklayers were well into their project, a young local woman passed through the tunnel as a shortcut to her home. Afraid of the bricklayers, Dixon let her take refuge in the company shack where he stood watch until the workers had left for the day. When the coast was clear, Dixon let the girl go on her way home, free of any anxiety from the bricklayers, but some say that the bricklayers had been watching Dixon that day — his body was found the next day lying in the tunnel beaten and bloody. His death was attributed to the jealous bricklayers working in the tunnel, presumably angry at how he interfered with whatever plans they had for the girl. Although the workers were suspected in the crime, nothing was ever done by local authorities to uncover the truth.

The Daring Teens

A second legend about the tunnels takes place years after Dixon's murder. By then the tunnel was finished and had become a popular hangout for teenagers in the area. Whenever a train approached, the teens would dart to the niches inside the tunnel to escape the danger of being hit. However, some children liked to play 'chicken' and only make it to the safety of the tunnel walls at the last second. One night, while the teens were gathered in the tunnel, a passenger train approached. The teens scattered to the walls, but this time their traditional safe haven would fail them, for as the train sped through, debris fell on the track and derailed the entire massive steel load. The accident killed all the passengers on board as well as the teens unlucky enough to still be in the tunnel at the time, unable to escape from the out-of-control train cars.

The Frightened Little Girl

The final legend associated with the train tunnel has to do with a little girl who was playing in the tunnel one summer day. The tunnel looks like a fun place to explore, which was exactly what the young girl was doing when the steel freight train came barreling through. Surprised by the sudden presence of the train and scared by its thundering sounds, the girl froze in the middle of the track. Some say she was sucked under the train while others say she was hit, but both accounts agree that she was killed in the tunnel that day.

The Ghosts

Popular legend has it that many ghosts haunt the Tunnelton Tunnel as lights floating along the tracks, much akin to wil-o-whips. It is said that if you walk along the tracks at night, Dixon will appear before you carrying a lantern as he makes his way down the tracks. Some people take this as a warning against an oncoming train while others think he is merely continuing with his route, checking for debris, as he did in life. It is also said that if you visit the tunnel at midnight spectators can see Dixon walking, his lantern light bobbing in the dark as he walks.

The ghosts of the children have also been seen darting along the walls as shadows in the tunnel. Sometimes shadow people have even been spotted outside the tunnel by curiosity seekers. They say the souls are of those who were lost walking through the tunnel and were killed by oncoming trains, unaware that they have ever died. Many of these shadow people are suspected to be the children who played chicken in the tunnel before the horrible accident, or maybe the ghost of the curious girl who was hit so many years ago.

Reflections

Although the tales are certainly interesting and have attracted onlookers for decades to the tunnel, only one of them can be validated. The tale of Dixon and his untimely death really did happen. According to Dixon's great-nephew, he did indeed die in a beating in the tunnel, but when asked about the sightings of seeing his great-uncle in the tunnel, the great-nephew would not comment.

The tale of the train wreck and the ghostly children who play in the tunnel, however, seems to be just local ghost lore. The accident can't be verified by any local newspapers or local records to ever have occurred. It is possible that a very real train wreck could have been mistakenly attributed to the Tunnelton Tunnel. One thing that will occur, however, is being arrested if you are caught exploring the tunnel at any time. Currently there is security present at the tunnel to keep the public away from the active train track. This track is still in use and the CSX Railroad Company probably doesn't want people wandering around where it is dangerous. So in the end the stories of the Tunnelton Tunnel have been and will remain local legends. However, it does teach a good lesson: stay out of places where you do not belong, or perhaps an unforeseeable tragedy may happen to you!

A destination for urban explorers and paranormal enthusiasts alike, the Tunnelton Tunnel is a very creepy place to visit. *Illustration by Kat Klockow.*

THE MYSTERIOUS BUSKIRK-SHOWERS MANSION

One of the most talked about "haunted" locations in Bloomington is that of the old Buskirk-Showers Mansion, better known as the former Portico's Restaurant building. Although no longer open to the public, the historic Edwardian-age mansion has found its niche in local lore because of the reports by former employees and restaurant guests about ghostly apparitions and bizarre noises. For years, when Portico's Restaurant was open, it entertained guests with fine food and happy times. However, this old mansion harbors a ghost or two that could tell another tale....

Haunting History

The property located at 520 North Walnut Street has had a long and complicated past. It is speculated that its history started in the early nineteenth century with a family that had a two-story home. Tragically, it is thought that the home was destroyed by a fire, killing the entire family, which included two young children. However, there are no records of a home there or a family living on the land before the mansion was built. After being cleared, the property remained vacant for years until it was eventually sold, in 1900, to Philip K. Buskirk, who built a luxurious 12,000-square foot mansion for his family known as Buskirk Mansion.

For seven years the family lived happily in their new home until tragedy struck Philip at the age of 44. While eating lunch with his family on August 22, 1907, Philip suddenly stiffened, fell forwards, and died in his chair. After

The old location for Portico's Restaurant, now the Buskirk-Showers Mansion, houses one of Bloomington's greatest paranormal mysteries.

Philip's death, the house fell out of the Buskirk family's hands and was held by a number of new owners until it was bought by William Showers, who owned a local furniture factory. Showers remodeled the home in 1915, making the first floor more spacious. The Showers family eventually sold the property in the 1940s to the Phi Kappa Tau Fraternity. When the fraternity relocated to a closer property on campus (the current Career Development Center), the now dubbed Buskirk-Showers Mansion was transformed into the Toad Hall furniture store, which remained in operation there until sometime in the 1970s. It was then sold again and transformed into a restaurant. The new restaurant's name was The Whimples, and it was at this time that paranormal activity started to be reported.

Tales of the Paranormal

Reports of the paranormal started with the opening of Whimples Restaurant. One night, shortly after the Whimples had opened, the staff was setting up for a formal banquet that was to take place the next afternoon. After most of the preparation was done, the only member of staff left to lock up the building was the restaurant manager. When the manager left the banquet room, all the table dressings were set and ready for the guests the next day. However, when the restaurant manger arrived the next morning, a curious situation was laid out before him — while the place settings were still in perfect order, on every table the wine glasses had been individually smashed into a pile of small glass pieces.

In 1980, Dr. Steven Lewallen and his wife Anita purchased the restaurant in the Buskirk-Showers Mansion and renamed it Portico's, a fine dining establishment in the heart of Bloomington. It quickly became a popular restaurant, but it may have become so for the spirits it held *in addition* to the fine wine list the restaurant offered. Unexplained phenomenon seemed to become commonplace on the premises, with some of the most chilling occurrences taking place in the women's restroom on the second floor. Repeated accounts tell of female patrons looking in the restroom's mirror only to see a young girl standing behind them, looking back at them. Other women reported being locked in the stalls by invisible forces for several minutes at a time. The men's restroom was not spared either: the sound of running water when nothing was turned on was reported. A plumber was called in to look into the matter, but he found everything dry and the water lines capped normally.

One evening, a female patron was climbing up the staircase on her way to the women's restroom when she was greeted by a spectral obstacle — a set of children that would not let her pass by them. She quickly returned to the main dining room to report the misbehaving children to Anita Lewallen, who rushed to the stairwell to shoo the children away, but didn't find them there...or anywhere else in the building. Children blocking the staircase has been reported by various visitors through the years, most mistaking the apparitions as being flesh and blood since they do not appear transparent. The ghosts have been described as being either a set of twin girls or a young brother and sister dressed in Victorian period clothing. By the time Anita or any other manager come to find the ghostly children, they have long vanished into the atmosphere.

Patrons would also complain to management about children making a racket upstairs above the dining room. More than once dinner guests would approach the owners and ask, "Are those your kids playing upstairs? We saw them bouncing a ball." The children, of course, would disappear after being reported. Staff and patrons have also reported hearing children say "Mommy" or "Come play with us, Mommy" on the second floor of the mansion.

Hearing the children's voices was a common occurrence that no one expected. Besides dinner guests hearing the children speak, on occasion the police would be called to the restaurant when the sound-activated security system would go off. Bloomington authorities would call the couple in the middle of the night reporting the sound of children playing with a ball in the upstairs hallway. Sometimes their voices were recorded saying ,"Mommy, Daddy, come play with us." The police would search every room looking for the children they had recorded talking...only to find the building empty.

In 1988, on Halloween, a radio host for WTTS-FM and WGTG-AM, Jerry Castor, decided that he would spend the night locked up in the "haunted" Buskirk-Showers Mansion. He had heard the tales from patrons and employees and was eager to experience the unexplained for himself. Although he didn't encounter an apparition when he spent the night, he did wake up with a surprise the next day! After making sure the entire building was secure in the evening, Castor settled down to work on recording some sound bites. While working on an audio recording, he fell asleep, leaving the device running. In the morning, he replayed the tape: among the sounds of him snoring, he clearly heard a young girl talking in the room with him. According to Caster, the girl on the recording said either, "Go spot" or "Cold spot," or perhaps even "No Spot!" After reviewing the four and a half hours of tape, Caster also found a short piece where he could hear what sounded like children running on the floor around him. He could not explain how this could have happened since he was sure he was the only *living* person in the building that night.

Similar to the experiences that the restaurant manager had at the Whimples, the Portico's manager and staff walked into a dining room completely ransacked without an apparent cause. According to the manger, after the last dinner guests had left, the staff went on to clean up the restaurant for the next day's service. Three waiters were present with the manager, locking the doors and counting up the day's receipts; none of them went into the main dining room. When the manager did, he found all the dishes and glasses broken and chairs strewn around the room haphazardly. The strange thing was that not one of the four men present in the building had heard a thing.

Another anomaly that has occurred in the building is the residual sight of the second floor burning. One evening in the late 1980s, after the restaurant had closed for the night, a passerby reported a fire on the second story to the Bloomington Fire Department. After rushing over to the building and contacting the Lewallens, the fire department discovered smoke in the building, but there was no fire to cause it.

The phenomenon of the "burning backs" was another anomaly to occur in the building. According to accounts, a waiter and waitress who were taking a short break from a busy evening in the dining room sat down on a couch in the upstairs hallway. After about a minute relaxing, the pair suddenly jumped up and started reaching for their backs. The waitress insisted that her back was burning...like a small fire had been lit right at the small of her back. It was even hot to the touch! The waiter also reported feeling a hot sensation while sitting on the couch, but after searching for the cause, he could not determine how the sofa had reached such temperatures. It was not positioned near a radiator or heating system of any means.

The Finale

After twelve years in operation, Portico's Restaurant closed in 1992. In 1995, the Buskirk-Showers Mansion was purchased by Pinnacle Properties Management Group, and they remain in the building to this day. The current owners do not favor visitors to the mansion looking for ghosts, nor have they reported any new accounts of a haunting in the years since they have been there. It would seem that the paranormal heyday of the Buskirk-Showers Mansion was also the restaurant's heyday — now it has gone into urban legend history for its haunted location.

When asked about the stories from the mansion, Anita Lewallen said she still wasn't a believer in ghosts, but that some of the occurrences reported in her restaurant were curious. At the time she would not mind any type of investigation being done in the building, but unfortunately that was never done before the property changed hands.

Reflections

The haunting of the Buskirk-Showers Mansion has become somewhat well known to local paranormal groups. Between stories reported in the newspapers, books, and the Internet, there seems to be more curiosity about the stories now than there ever was before. I couldn't get a hold of the current property owners to get their comments on the supposed haunting, but they have made it clear to interested parties that no paranormal investigations are desired. The events that took place from 1970 to 1992 remain a mystery to the population outside the building — and only time will tell what secrets lay inside.

MORGAN-MONROE
STATE FOREST

If you are driving down US 37 between Martinsville and Bloomington, no doubt you have seen the entrances to Morgan-Monroe State Forest. Most drivers speeding through the area don't bother to turn down Turkey Track Road and follow the numerous twists and turns needed to find themselves at the main entrance of the park. One can easily get lost among the 23,465 acres of wilderness seemingly in the middle of nowhere, but like many other locations highlighted in this book, Morgan-Monroe State Park's existence is telling of Indiana's history as a state. Step inside the boundaries of Morgan-Monroe's Stepp Cemetery and the secrets of history will whisper to you.

Haunting History

Indiana formally became the nineteenth state to join the Union on December 11, 1816. With the creation of the state meant the creation of counties. Monroe County, where Bloomington and Indiana University are located, was established in 1818. Meanwhile, Morgan County, of which Martinsville is the county seat, was established in 1821 from parts of neighboring Delaware and Wabash counties. The area was quickly settled before either county was officially created by eager farmers settling Indiana...one such family was the Stepps.

Reuben Stepp moved his family of nine to Central Indiana from North Carolina in 1859, purchasing land that included parts of the current state forest. On their new farm, the Stepp family raised corn and pigs while carving their niche into the Indiana countryside. Reuben had a small log cabin church built on his property to serve the needs of the local community. Through the years, it became necessary to have a cemetery, and Stepp Cemetery was created near the church. In 1884, Reuben Stepp moved to Texas, selling the property to Will Peterson, who, in turn, sold the property to Fred Walls, who owned the land until 1929. Members from all of the families who owned the land are buried in the cemetery, although most of their headstones are long gone.

By the mid-1920s most farmers had abandoned their homesteads in the area due to rocky soil and poor farming conditions. In 1929, Morgan-Monroe State Forest was established to stem the growing erosion problem from decades of farming and deforestation. Stepp Cemetery is actually

This photo shows the distance from **Baby Lester's** grave to the current tree stump in **Stepp Cemetery**... It's not very convenient for singing lullabies, is it?

Pennies are tossed onto Baby Lester's grave in hopes that its mother would invisibly throw them off.

one of six family cemeteries within the state forest, a fact that confuses many visitors looking for the particularly infamous Stepp Cemetery.

Spooky Stories

So what is the attraction to Stepp Cemetery? It is an old, small, and isolated pioneer cemetery located in the middle of a huge state forest that is not easy to find unless you know where to look. The answer is because of the legends, of course...particularly the story of the Lady in Black and her "witch's throne." As the legend traditionally goes, a young wife and mother traumatically lost her husband and baby boy in a car accident around the 1890s. She had her family buried in Stepp Cemetery where she visited them every night at midnight wearing a completely black ensemble of clothing. As she aged, she grew more and more reclusive from the world around her, shying away from contact with outsiders to the point where she would run away from anyone who approached her. She sat on her tree stump, known as the "witch's throne" or "warlock's seat," rocking and singing lullabies to her deceased baby. The witch's throne, as rumor had it, was created when lightning struck a tree causing it to fall, leaving

This tree stump in Stepp Cemetery has been attributed to the "Lady in Black" myth.

a chair-like form behind. The mother eventually passed away and was buried next to her family in an unmarked grave by the townsfolk. Now legend has it that if someone was to sit in the chair during a full moon at midnight, they would be cursed to die within the year.

This version of the story of the Lady in Black has been around since the early 1900s, but another popular legend sets the story in the rock'n 1950s. In this second version, the young mother loses her husband to an accident in the limestone quarry where he worked in the 1930s and buried him in Stepp Cemetery. Now a single parent to a daughter, the mother becomes obsessed with her child's security, doting on her precious child's every need while keeping her under strict control. Eventually the daughter blossoms into a beautiful teenager who attracts the attention of the local boys. She is asked to a spring school dance by a charming boy at school and begs her mother to let her go with him. The mother relents under the condition that the girl be home by 10 p.m. that evening or face further isolation from society.

The night of the dance arrived and the girl goes off for an enjoyable night at the school dance free from her mother's control. While the pair dance the evening away, a typical spring shower rains down on the Bloomington countryside causing the oil to rise from the asphalt. Time flew by as they danced, the young couple not realizing that they had only a few minutes to get the girl home before her curfew would pass. The couple raced back to her house in the boy's car hoping to make it to the house on time, driving way too fast for the tight twists and turns through the landscape. Just a short distance from their goal, the young man lost control of his car and careened into a tree, killing him instantly and sending the girl sailing through the windshield and into the air. According to the legend, she lost her head from a fence wire as she flew through the air. The couple was buried in Stepp Cemetery within their family's plots. The mother, distraught with the premature death of her only child, vowed to wear nothing but black for the rest of her life. She visited the cemetery every night sitting on a tree stump talking to her family's graves. Eventually the mother went insane with the solitude and was taken to a mental institution (maybe Central State Hospital), where she later died. She was buried next to her family in an unmarked grave by the townsfolk.

These are only two versions of the very popular Indiana legend. From what I could find, there are roughly thirteen different versions documented in various books, newspapers, or on the Internet, but what is the most interesting is the manner of the haunting within the cemetery. The Lady in Black receives her name from the black outfit that she has been described wearing; it covers all but her face and hands. Her ghost is said to be an attractive older woman with long silver hair and is commonly seen walking along the headstones or sitting down on the stump singing to a gravestone engraved with the inscription "Baby Lester 1937." If noticed, she will dart from view into the darkness of the woods.

The Lady in Black of Stepp Cemetery is also the subject of many "parking" legends from the mid-twentieth century, particularly from the 1960s. According to one such legend, the Lady in Black will appear to young couples parked in the woods for some private time. She will knock on the doors of the car holding the bloody and bruised head of her daughter in her arms or on a chain around her neck. In another version, she has gained a steel hook for a right hand, a variation of the "Hook" urban legend popular in the 1960s and 70s. She even has appeared as a black spectral dog guarding the grave of Baby Lester. All of these urban legends originate with the central character of the Lady in Black.

For all the popularity of Stepp Cemetery, it is not the only paranormal location in the state forest. Some reports have recounted the story of two brothers who once lived on land now covered in the territory of the forest line. As the legend goes, the two men were sons of a wealthy landowner back in the early 1800s. After the father died, the two brothers were in control of his land, but failed to agree on any issue regarding what to do with it. The arguing came to a head one day, resulting with the brothers dueling in a pistol match. Both men managed to inflict fatal wounds on each other and were buried next to their father in a local cemetery nearby, but they seemed to not have rested in peace. According to local lore, hikers traveling through the woods have run into the arguing brothers, only to watch them fade away into the background when approached. Other reports have mentioned cars dying in the vicinity of the haunting, starting up again after a minute or two for no apparent reason. It should be noted that this story has been reported to take place in both Morgan-Monroe Start Forest and Hoosier National Forest just down the road on State Road 37. Both forests reside on previous cropland, so the story can be plausible in both locations.

Spooky Story Spoilers!

I do have some spoilers for those who believe the stories concerning Stepp Cemetery. If you are a fan of these stories and don't want to find out the real facts about the cemetery, then dear reader stop reading now. However, if you are an individual who loves to know anything that can be found out about a location, then please continue....

The Benton Township Trustees, as of August 2001, maintain Stepp Cemetery, so it is anything but an "abandoned" cemetery as many visitors think. For over a century the cemetery was in use, with records showing the peak for internments from the 1870s to the 1980s. There are several war veterans buried in the cemetery, including a Confederate soldier from the Civil War. For nearly seventy years, the Walls family, who owned the land before the state purchased it, took care of the cemetery. The family is responsible for removing the old log cabin church that, after time and disuse, had rotted away. In addition, they were the ones who commissioned the Stepp Cemetery stone sign to be engraved and placed at the front of the cemetery.

The next surprise is that the "witch's throne" was the work of William and Ralph Walls, a pair of brothers who owned a saw mill and were caretakers of the cemetery for many years. In the early 1960s, the brothers took down a dying double tree located near Baby Lester's grave at the edge of the woods — and the legend of the "witch's throne" was born. When the tree had fallen, Ralph thought that the stump looked like a good seat for guests to use while visiting the cemetery so they left it where it was. Ralph then joked that the stump could be a seat for the ghost of the Lady in Black. Eventually this stump rotted away and was removed by William after Ralph died in 1981. He too is buried in Stepp Cemetery. So, in the end, the infamous stump was created by humans and removed by humans — there is absolutely nothing supernatural about the entire thing. Sorry folks!

Furthermore, the Lady in Black is really a man named John Findley. For a few weeks during the late summer of 1966, Findley and his friend Jack Abram "haunted" the cemetery. The two started their mischief by stringing a dummy dressed in a black dress with a large black floppy hat on a pulley system inside the graveyard. According to Findley's account, they had just put the finishing touches on the dressed dummy's pulley system when a car full of teenagers pulled off the road near the cemetery. Findley and Abram positioned the dummy so it looked as if someone was standing under a tree and, as the teenagers got out of the car, they walked the dummy towards them. The teens, scared at what they were witnessing, jumped back into their old car and sped off, with one brave teen attempting to throw a coke bottle at the figure on his way out.

Another prank Findley and Abram pulled was to rig a bush with wire so they could make it move when the wire was pulled to startle visitors. When they pulled the wire to make the bush shake, the two men would simultaneously howl like wolves. An article circa August 30, 1966 from the *Herald Times* mentions the mysterious Lady in Black legend after a couple of teenage boys hung a dog in the cemetery. The young teens who hung the dog claimed they found it dead on the side of the road and thought it would be amusing to hang it in a tree. The teens were promptly rounded up by police for questioning.

Findley and Abram were not the only pranksters to "haunt" the cemetery; many members of the Walls family "haunted" the cemetery from time to time. Young members of the Walls family have admitted that they would take great fun from hiding in the bushes around the cemetery and scaring trespassers at night. This prank is something the family now regrets because it only served to increase the amount of visitors and vandalism to the cemetery.

Baby Lester's grave has received a lot of attention over the years. One legend states that if someone was to place a penny on his gravestone, the Lady in Black would throw it off using her invisible hands. Paranormally speaking this is a remarkable feat...too bad it is the stuff of urban legends. Baby Lester, in truth, was the stillborn son of Harley Lester and his wife Olethia Walls in 1937. Although it is an interesting tale about how Baby Lester's mother visited him nightly and threw pennies off the grave marker, it couldn't be true since Olethia Walls passed away at the age of eighty-five in 2007. She joked about the urban legend in life, stating that although she had white hair, she rarely ever wore black.

Skulls and Candles

There have also been reports of occult activity in the area for over a century, with many of the stories taking place in Stepp Cemetery. One such report is about the Crabbites, a small group of occult enthusiasts who practiced group orgies and other occult rituals in the confines of the cemetery. Since that time there have been a handful of occult groups that make pilgrimages to the cemetery to practice their rituals. Evidence shows that many rituals are focused around the stump in the center of the cemetery. When I visited the cemetery in January 2009, I found fresh candle wax on the center tree stump. Paranormal groups have found other evidence of candles being placed on various headstones in the cemetery, one of the most popular being the angel monument. Witnesses have also reported seeing people urinating on the tree stump, so I highly suggest people watch where they are sitting while visiting Stepp Cemetery.

The Investigations

Morgan-Monroe State Forest really does have a knack to attract ghosts. Maybe this is due to the numerous cemeteries within it. Stepp Cemetery has attracted most of the attention through the years, especially for ghost hunters. Both amateurs and experienced investigators travel to Stepp Cemetery to investigate the alleged haunting. Groups such as Indiana Ghost Trackers, Hoosier Paranormal, Midwestern Researchers and Investigators of Paranormal Activity, the Phantom Tribe, and countless other groups have all investigated the cemetery with varying amounts of "success." Common phenomena reported by the groups are cold spots around the cemetery, members being followed by the sound of footsteps, and bizarre red anomalies such as orbs and mists in photos taken in the cemetery. Strange noises while investigating the area have also been reported, but it is difficult to say if they were natural or not.

Members of IGT have looked into the cemetery's haunting multiple times through the years. Chapters from Indianapolis and Bloomington are the most frequent visitors due to its close proximity. Lisa, the current Regional Director of IGT, had an interesting run-in with an apparition while on one of her first hunts with the group. Many years ago before she became an officer, the Bloomington Chapter traveled to the cemetery for a public hunt. While the group was in the middle of an EVP session, Lisa saw what she described to be a white form, about three feet tall, run through the group's circle and between the legs of Bill, a fellow investigator. According to Lisa's story, she cupped her hands over her mouth to prevent making any noise during the EVP session. Others in the group noticed her ruckus, with Bill turning to her and saying, "You saw it too?" The group also heard strange noises and footsteps as they continued to investigate the cemetery throughout the night.

On a different occasion, a fellow IGT member from the Indianapolis chapter had a haunting experience of her own. While investigating the cemetery one evening, Elizabeth took a series of photographs of the woods surrounding it — what the photos produced was alarming....

Elizabeth has no way to explain these photographs. According to her, there were no other people in the cemetery at the time they investigated and the camera's flash failed to shoot. These light sources seem to emit their own red glow, which may explain why the camera's flash trigger was not activated.

Streaks of light are photographed in Stepp Cemetery (in the top corners of the frame)... the cause of them is unknown. *Courtesy of Elizabeth Wynn.*

Desecration

IGT Bloomington seems to be one of the lucky groups to have experienced something strange; most groups report no activity during their investigations the cemetery. Many times groups are interrupted while looking into the activity at Stepp Cemetery by either other paranormal groups or curiosity seekers attempting their own brand of "ghost hunting."

Unwelcome visitors are common and vandals have desecrated the gate walls of the cemetery as well as toppled over century-old grave markers and defaced all but one of the original headstones. Many times headstones have been found in random places around the county: along the hiking trails within

Looking closely at this photo some see the silhouette of a farmer waving from just outside the cemetery's boundaries. Could this be Reuben Stepp?
Courtesy of Elizabeth Wynn.

the state forest, in various parking lots of local businesses, and even Martinsville High School. The headstones have always managed to be returned to the cemetery, however sometimes the damage done is irreversible.

Reflections

In the end, the stories from Stepp Cemetery are just that...*stories*. However, the legends don't necessarily explain why some groups that have visited the cemetery have seen and felt unexplainable things.

History doesn't account for a lot of the activity said to take place in Stepp Cemetery; for example, there are no written records about the Crabbite's antics. The story of the Crabbites seems to be an oral narrative shared around the population, maybe in an attempt to deter curious folk from coming to the cemetery.

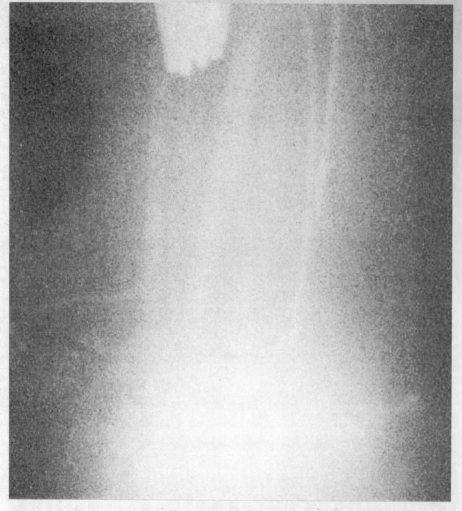

The cause of this aura (which is red in the actual photograph) in Stepp Cemetery is unknown. Could it be more evidence of the paranormal? *Courtesy of Elizabeth Wynn.*

In addition, the legend of the Lady in Black seems to have been well known before the 1960s to already draw a crowd and be cited in old newspaper articles. It could very well be that the legend from the 1960s has been superimposed onto the legend from 1890, creating an entirely different story. Her legend caught the attention of Jack Auburn and John Findley enough to impersonate her. Not to forget Walls and their antics in the cemetery in the 1970s. Perhaps the Lady in Black is a different woman who suffered a tragic end? Or the spectral dog mentioned in some legends is that of the dog hung in the tree in 1966? Although the traditional stories have been debunked, it only conjures up new questions about the activity that has been recorded.

My personal opinion is that Stepp Cemetery is not as active as the legends make it out to be. Truly the legends about the Lady in Black have created such a sensation that curiosity seekers have taken the trouble of finding Stepp Cemetery for a night of frightening fun. If you look on Google Maps, Stepp Cemetery is listed as a haunted destination (this is actually how I found directions to it). Speaking as a paranormal investigator, a cemetery — or any outdoor hunt location for that matter — is a terrible place to run an investigation unless you know what you are doing. Dust, pollen, and bugs can pollute photos and cause a whole host of "false positives" that get toted around the Internet as "proof" that paranormal events take place at the cemetery. This only serves to keep the cycle of abuse to Stepp Cemetery rolling, which so many, like myself, would like to stop.

The author sits next to the stone sign that the Walls Family commissioned to greet visitors to the old cemetery. *Photo by Mike Klockow.*

THE SHADOW PEOPLE
OF SPRING MILL

Nestled in the midst of the rolling hills of southern Indiana is Spring Mill State Park. Located three miles east of Mitchell, Spring Mill offers a variety of outdoor activities and historic attractions to wet any historian's or outdoor enthusiast's appetite. The state park is home to four caves: Broson, Twin, Shawnee (also known as Donald's Cave), and Hamer, in addition to other geological attractions such as sinkholes. Visitors can stroll through the pioneer village, take a boat tour through Twin Caves, explore Donaldson Woods, or visit Mitchell Karst Plain Nature Preserves, which houses a forest full of virgin wood. And, if you have time at the end of the day, stop by a haunted graveyard.

Haunting History

Before the state park was established, the area was home to a small pioneer village that flourished in the mid to late 1800s. This village occupied 295 acres of the hilly and forested Indiana landscape. The first building to be completed on the land was a grain mill in 1817, which still stands and works to this day. In the late 1800s, the Baltimore and Ohio Railroad was completed, but the small village was bypassed as a stop on the train route. Because of this, commerce dropped, villagers moved out, and the once-bustling village became a ghost town.

The land that the village occupied was then purchased for a single dollar by a cement company. However, nothing seems to have been done to the area, leaving the old village falling apart as the decades trudged by. Richard Lieber, an Indiana businessman and founder of the Indiana State Parks system, acquired the land with E.Y. Guernsey and started to reconstruct the old pioneer village on the old site in an attempt to bring Indiana's pioneer history back to life. The reconstructed village contains six original log or limestone buildings that were restored on site, but today there are seven: the old gristmill (1817), the mill office (1818), the sawmill (1823), the nursery and school (1830), spring house (1840), and finally the apothecary (1830), which houses artifacts donated by Eli Lilly of Eli Lilly and Company pharmaceuticals.

Six reconstructions of log buildings were also built on the site when the village was reconstructed: the distillery and workshop (1932), the lower residence (1935), the summer kitchen, the carriage house, and the blacksmith shop (1931), and the old stagecoach trail. Later the meeting house (1976) was completed. Originally four log buildings were also relocated to the pioneer village, but today it has grown to six buildings. The old structures are from other locations around the state when the original buildings were in such poor condition they couldn't be restored: the weaver's shop (1816 cabin of the Sheeks family), Granny White House (1824), the tavern (1824), pottery shop (1820s), garden cabin (1830), and the upper residence (1820).

Today, there is also a company of "interpreters," or actors, recreating daily life in the community, on hand to answer visitors' questions about life during the pioneering days of Indiana. These actors are dressed in the style of those who lived in the village in the early 1800s. The purpose of this is to let visitors feel completely immersed in the daily lives of those in the 1800s, so guests can feel like they have stepped back in time to visit those who settled Indiana.

Located within the state park is the Virgil I. "Gus" Grissom memorial, dedicated to the second American to fly through space. A Mitchell, Indiana, native and a member of the Mercury-Redstone 4, Gemini III space missions, Gus Grissom was tragically killed in a test launch of Apollo I with Ed White and Roger Chaffee in 1967. Because of his accomplishments, Grissom has become a local hero. The Gemini III space capsule, his space suit, and a short documentary on his life can be seen in the memorial building.

South of the Pioneer Village is Hamer Cemetery, the original graveyard for the old village. Headstones within the cemetery are a jumble of old and new, with some dating back to the 1860s; some are more recent, belonging to relatives of the original settling pioneer families.

Ghostly Legends

Through the decades that Spring Mill State Park has been in operation, two locations in the park have gained an association with the paranormal — Hamer Cemetery and the old pioneer village.

Hamer Cemetery

Home to a shadowy figure of a man said to have been murdered because of an outstanding gambling debt, according to legend, the man died destitute. Because of this, nothing was engraved on his headstone, so it was erected blank in the graveyard. The ghostly figure of the man is said to appear every night before his bare headstone — and makes a ritual of walking to the grave of the man who killed him. Conveniently enough, this grave is located in the same cemetery!

The Pioneer Village

Moving north into the pioneer village, visitors have reported seeing a variety of ghostly activity at night after the park has closed. Odd, unexplained lights have been witnessed floating alongside the buildings and full-bodied figures have been seen walking inside the log buildings. Other visitors have reported seeing shadow people walking along the pathways to the old mill and looking out the windows from inside the building.

Reflections

Who is it that haunts the old pioneer village and Hamer Cemetery? The truth may never be fully understood. The apparition in Hamer Cemetery remains nameless, and tales about the ghost never mention the name of the man who supposedly killed him even though he walks to his headstone. In my opinion, the ghosts of Spring Mill State Park are not intelligent ghosts that would interact with visitors, but are a residual haunting. These phantoms are unaware of the living visiting the area and are not harmful in the least. They are nothing to be afraid of, so sit back and watch the true interpreters show you what life was like in the early days of the state's history.

CRUMP THEATER'S
FANTASTIC PHANTOMS

Located thirty-eight miles east of Bloomington on State Road 46 is the city of Columbus, Indiana. Originally named "Tiptonia" in 1820 after General Jon Tipton, who owned the land and forests in the area, the city was renamed "Columbus" March, 20 1821. The city is the county seat of Bartholomew County, the same county that Azalia and its haunted bridge are located in. Columbus is also very well known (and proud of) its wide variety of modern architecture. When you have notable architects such as I.M. Pei, Richard Meier, and Eero Saarinen designing the city's public libraries, bridges, schools, and churches, you would be proud too! One such wonder of architecture, at least in its day, is the Crump Theater on Third Street in downtown Columbus. It has had a rocky history to say the least, as it has seen the population through two World Wars, the rise of modern architecture, and just barely escaped demolition. The Crump has the charm of a by-gone era, but not all of its past guests have left for good it seems.

The History

Something funny about the Crump Theater is that its exact date of establishment is largely unknown. It is suspected that the theater was established between the years of 1872 and 1874; most sources credit John A. Keith, a local attorney, with establishing the theater in 1874. However, in 1872, the Columbus newspaper, *The Republic*, noted a theater being built that even had a tenant for the first floor space. Sources also identify the opera house under two names — Crump's Opera Hall or J.S. Crump's New Theater — but regardless of the name, the theater was the first opera house in Columbus. The building was met with excitement, and much was written about the fine wood carvings and detail work put into the façade of the building's interior and exterior.

The year 1889 was a big year for the theater; the new detail work on the building was finally finished and it gained new owners, the Crump family. However, the appearance of the finished building looked different from how it was originally planned a decade before. As the decades passed and a new century turned, the opera stage saw Vaudeville Theater troops become dominant and opera shows were pushed out of touring. On May 6, 1914, audiences in the city were introduced to something new — "moving pictures."

John Crump, the last Crump to own the theater, passed away in 1918, although the theater still holds the family's name. The building was closed for renovations for two years after that, opening to the public in 1920 with a new

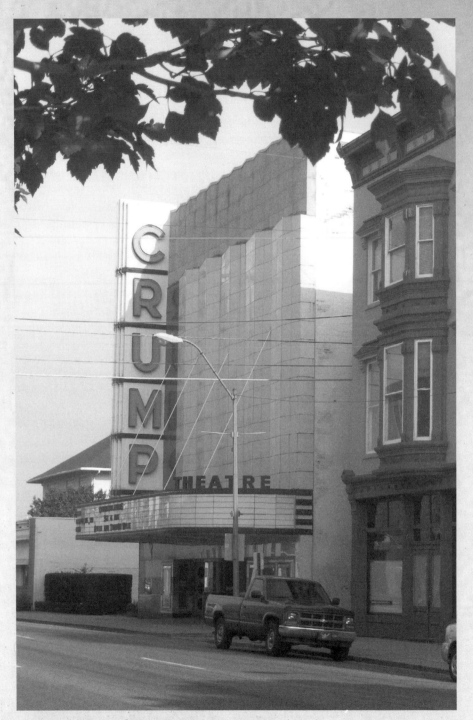

The front marquee of Crump Theater...

façade and a stage fitted to allow both Vaudeville and cinema shows. By 1941, the Crump Theater had changed hands twice and underwent another facelift to "modernize" the building. The modern facelift featured a new exterior of cream stucco and Vitrolite glass front doors and the interior was remolded with vinyl wall coverings and built-in couches, but the Crump's crowning glory was the new marquee installed on the front. Standing at forty-five feet and spelling out the five shining letters of "C-R-U-M-P," the marquee has become a Columbus landmark. The Crump, like the rest of downtown Columbus, saw its heyday through the 1940s to the late 1960s before the modern malls in the suburbs of the city sprang up in the 1970s. In the 1980s, the Crump slowly declined into a dollar theater, and the building battled ever-increasing decay before finally closing its doors in 1987. Many lifetime residents of Columbus thought that the Crump's lights had gone out forever.

Thanks to the efforts of many concerned citizens, however, the old Crump Theater is still up and running! Vernon Jewel purchased the theater in 1989 to prevent the building from being torn down; five years later the Columbus Capital Foundation, on behalf of Historic Columbus Development, purchased the building. The Crump Theater serves as a stage for local talent to perform and even has hosted a rock concert by famous Indiana musician John Mellencamp — events that make this theater stand out from the rest. Volunteers take time out of their week to help clean, fix up, and mend decades of neglect from the seats and walls of the old building.

Since 2002 Rovene Quigley has been the Project and Facilities Director of Crump Theater for the Columbus Capital Foundation. Currently, besides donations made to the Crump, the Heritage Fund is the only source of financial assistance for the old theater. Quigley has opened up the theater for Friday night rock shows, is responsible for the return of live theater to the stage, and has allowed ghost hunters into the building to investigate the stories of alleged spirits roaming the halls (as long as they don't mess with the light bulbs). The year 2008 saw the beginning of the annual Indiana PhenomeCon, a local paranormal convention hosted by paranormal investigative groups from around the state.

The Ghost Stories

Looking at the ghost stories that have accumulated over the years, this is one of the few locations where interactive or intelligent spirits outnumber the residual ghosts of decades past. Many visitors to the building have felt the chilling presence of the Crump's phantoms, although few have actually seen them. One of the commonly perceived phenomena is hearing "old time" music flowing from the mezzanine level down the front staircases of the building, but when the music has been investigated, no cause could be found. Phantom fragrances have also been detected around the building, sometimes following visitors as they walk around the theater. Claims made that objects move about by unseen forces is central in two stories from Rovene Quigley about her helpful ghosts.

Quigley's first story involves the boiler in the building. A few years ago the boiler started having issues that required Quigley to find the inspection certificates for the system. After searching the old offices and subsequently the rest of the building, she failed to find the certificates and left the Crump distraught about the missing documents. The next day she gloomily returned to the building...to find the required inspection documents laying haphazardly in the middle of the stage! Quigley credits the ghosts of Crump Theater for finding the documents for her, thinking that perhaps they knew that without those documents, their home was in trouble.

The ghosts assisted Quigley again in 2006, this time financially. According to Quigley, one night after an event at the theater she was counting the money from the cash register. The end funds totaled $86.50, which she promptly stored inside a small popcorn bag to deliver to the Heritage Fund the following day. A week passed before she was confronted by a volunteer who had been going through the cash register after that weekend's event. The volunteer asked Quigley if she forgot about depositing the funds from the event, which Quigley responded she had not. The volunteer then showed her that she had found money in the register wrapped up in a popcorn bag...$86.50. Quigley called up the Heritage Fund to confirm that she had

The author talks to Rovene Quigley about the strange stories at Crump Theater.
Photo by Mike Klockow.

deposited the previous weekend's funds, which, in fact, she had. So this package of money literally came out of thin air. Quigley attributes the extra funds as donations from the ghosts...an act to keep their home intact.

Apparitions have also been reported on the staircase to the mezzanine floor from the lobby and in the upper seating of the balcony. Many visitors have claimed seeing an adult man with a child on the staircase leading up to the guest lounges on the second floor. One such incident was told to me by Lisa Bradley, the director of Indiana Ghost Trackers (IGT) Bloomington chapter.

In April 2009, the second annual Indiana PhenomeCon was held at Crump Theater. Lisa had brought her young son with her to prepare for the next day's festivities at the theater along with fellow IGT officer Melanie Hunter who was helping to set up the Indiana Ghost Trackers booth. The booth was located on the mezzanine lobby of the theater and, while setting up, Lisa's son suddenly started panicking and crying that there was a man on the stairs and that he was watching the group working. Lisa quickly exited the building with her son to comfort him, thinking that he had possibly seen one of the Crump's reported ghosts.

Later, during the night investigation conducted as part of the conference, Lisa and a team of other investigators examined the mezzanine lounges, located in a suite with the gentlemen's and ladies' restrooms. Some investigative groups have reported strange things occurring in either lounge area, which sparked Lisa's group's interest. During this time, Lisa snapped a picture of a mirror in one of the lounges...resulting in a photo of an apparition wearing a hat looking back at her! There was no way to explain the photo — no one in the group was wearing a hat or anything remotely like the silhouette in the picture. Perhaps this is a photo of the ghostly man who Lisa's son saw earlier that day.

The other mentioned hotspot of paranormal activity is the upper seating of the balcony where one particular apparition has been met multiple times through the years — the man in the brown suit. Today the balcony has been remolded to fit two storage rooms behind the fold down seats, flanking either side of the projection room, but before the storage rooms were created this area of the balcony was segregated seating for the "colored" members of the audience. The apparition keeps himself around the balcony as maybe a bitter memory of those days; visitors and investigators have reported meeting a transparent elderly black gentleman who wears a brown suit and fedora hat. He is courteous...nodding to the visitor before fading away into the inky darkness of the storage rooms. Strange electromagnetic spikes have been reported along with electronic voice phenomenon recorded by various groups. Knocks and cold spots have also been reported all over the balcony, not just in the storage room.

Rovene Quigley had a short story to share with me about the ghost up in the balcony. A few years ago there was a high school student who was visiting the Crump Theater to write a school paper about the historical site and its ghosts, much like my visit to the theater. Quigley was showing the teenage student the colored seating area of the balcony, which has duct work running along the sides and up above the storage rooms, telling him the story about the ghost of the man in the brown suit and all the experiences guests have had with him. When the student remarked, "I don't believe much in ghosts," there was a sudden loud banging coming from the duct work in the room. Quigley and the student rushed out of the room into the comforting glow of the balcony lights — and the student retracted his previous statement by saying, "Maybe I will now."

Probably the most well known story about the ghosts at Crump Theater doesn't involve the balcony or the second floor lounges; it is about the basement dressing rooms below the stage. Quigley explained that a pair of contracted electricians was visiting the theater to take readings on the electric wiring of the building. Their work led one of the men to go into the basement dressing rooms while Quigley and the other electrician talked on the stage floor above about the theater. The electrician didn't stay down in the basement long, shooting back up onto the stage a minute after going down there. According to him, he didn't feel welcome down there — and the hairs on his arms stood up on end as if some phantom presence was with him. He quickly gathered the data he needed before rushing back into the comfort of living companions. Quigley did mention that a few people have heard or seen the apparition of a teenage girl in the dressing room area of the Crump Theater. Her true identity has been lost in the sands of time, but she is believed to have been an actress in the early days of the theater.

The Investigations

Because of all the reported activity in the old theater, Crump is a popular location for paranormal groups to visit and investigate. In April 2009, I was lucky enough to join an IGT Indianapolis ghost hunt there. It was my first experience investigating an auditorium and at the time, and I didn't have plans to include the Crump in this book. It was a clear early April evening when the group met up under the large Crump marquee waiting to be welcomed into the lobby of the building. Rovene Quigley, dressed up as a 1920s flapper for a party she was attending later that night, met us and quickly gave the us a tour of the building while telling of other paranormal group's experiences and visitor's accounts of strange phenomena. Her dress fit the atmosphere of the old building, especially when she recounted the theater's remarkable history.

We shut off most of the lights in the building and split up our large group into two smaller groups to start the investigation. Upon entering the basement, I was immediately hit with the overwhelming odor of mildew. It had been a soggy spring in Indiana, and the mildew was strong in the damp basement. The hallway, framed by unfinished and bare beams, gave the feeling of walking through an old sanatorium such as Waverly Hills. Off to the side of the hallway were small chambers where stage actors once relaxed and put on their costumes before entering the stage floor above them. Now, odds and ends are stored in these rooms, including a wooden replica of an electric chair that Quigley made for the "haunted theater" tour one Halloween time, and the old windows have been bricked up. This is definitely not an area those who suffer from claustrophobia should visit.

While participating in an EVP session, the group did get a K2 hit when asked about taking pictures with the ghosts of Crump. However, the K2 meter never reacted like that again, even when we put electronics up to the meter such as holding a digital camera and taking a picture. After an hour, our time was up in the basement and we returned to the main stage via the back staircase. As we climbed the old stairs, many of the investigators, including myself, heard a faint whisper speak to us. It sounded like a young woman, but upon reviewing my digital recorder, nothing was recorded to back up what we heard.

Crump Theater's balcony is considered one of the hotspots for paranormal activity.

The stage left staircase is where many paranormal investigators have reportedly heard sounds of a girl talking.

This photo was taken during an Indiana Ghost Trackers investigation of Crump Theater. Could it be an image of one of the theater's ghosts in the mirror? *Courtesy of Lisa Bradley.*

The teams met up again in the lobby where the unused equipment was being stored while we were conducting investigations elsewhere in the building. The teams shared theories and discussed the old building's condition and the efforts being undertaken to save it while taking swigs of soda. After a couple of minutes passed, the teams separated again and this time mine was headed up to the balcony area. The other team arranged themselves in a dressing room located directly under the stage. Both teams were quiet as we began conducting EVP sessions. Our team separated into two smaller groups of three, each group taking a storage compartment where the former segregated seating once was located. My team was located in the storage room to the left of the projection room. While inside, one of the investigators thought they heard rain hitting the roof of the building, but it wasn't raining outside. We couldn't figure out what the cause of this phenomena was...perhaps it was a residual auditory event.

After fifteen minutes, both groups reunited on the center balcony to do one EVP session. We were sitting still, not making a sound in an attempt to soak in the environment and adjust our eyes before proceeding with an EVP session. Suddenly, a voice came over the walk-talkie our group leader had;

it was the other team's leader. "Stop talking so loudly," she spat, irritated that we were making so much noise and contaminating their data. "We're not talking," replied our team leader. A hush fell over the radio waves. The other team was apparently hearing something on the stage that we, in the balcony, were not hearing. It was about this time I was told later on that one of the team members in the basement had been grabbed in the back of the neck by a cold, unseen hand.

After reviewing the photographic and auditory data collected that night, I found nothing. There were a few dust orbs found floating through my pictures, but nothing that screamed out "paranormal." Other groups, however, had captured some very interesting footage and data from the old theater.

Other Investigations

Many other paranormal groups have investigated Crump Theater looking to disprove or provide evidence that the century-old theater's tales of the supernatural are indeed true. I talked to two such groups: Hoosier Paranormal Research and Midwest Researchers and Investigators of Paranormal Activity. Both groups have visited Crump Theater in a series of ongoing investigations, and so far the theater has done little to disappoint them.

Hoosier Paranormal Research (HPR) has visited Crump Theater twice, in February and December of 2006. Through the two investigations, the team has recorded quite a few EVPs of varying clarity. On their first investigation, they caught an EVP up in the balcony that seems to be the voice of a man saying, "What was that?" Since the first trip's data was inconclusive, the team returned ten months later, but this time in a joint effort with Quest Paranormal. With the teams spread out investigating the large building all at one time, they were able to cover more ground, which turned up more evidence. HPR caught a number of EVPs that night, but one stood out from the others. It is the EVP of a male voice saying, "Jump...jump." What is interesting about this EVP is that other guests to Crump Theater have witnessed what they described was the figure of a man running towards the edge of the balcony like he was going to jump off of it, only to disappear into thin air before jumping. It seems the group found evidence to correlate with that story.

Midwest Researchers and Investigators of Paranormal Activity (MRIPA) have also looked into the reports of paranormal activity at the Crump Theater, visiting three times since September of 2008. Although rare, MRIPA has concluded that Crump Theater is indeed haunted. What drove them to this conclusion is a very good video of a male figure on the balcony sitting down and then lounging in a seat for a minute before fading into the inky darkness. The footage can be seen on their website along with photos and other data collected during their investigations. Out of the hundred or so investigations listed on their website, only two have been labeled as haunted by the group — and one of them is the Crump Theater.

Reflections

It seems that many paranormal investigative teams believe Crump Theater is quite haunted by both residual energy and intelligent spirits wandering the premises. From looking at Lisa's photo evidence, the EVP evidence from Hoosier Paranormal Research, and the video evidence from MRIPA, it seems that the most prominent ghost actively roving the Crump Theater is that of a gentleman, but the question remains: Is more than one spirit haunting the theater? It is hard to tell since accounts of personal experiences and investigative data are reported all over the building, but it seems this ghost isn't too keen on others looking for him. The great question is what connection does this male ghost have to the theater? Was he once a patron? Was he once an actor? Or perhaps an employee of the theater at one time? No one seems to know.

What I think is that the ghost gives the Crump Theater a personal charm all its own. In regards to Rovene Quigley, the ghost seems to want to help her as much as possible. Perhaps the living could learn a lesson from the Crump Theater ghost...that this historic theater is an important landmark for the city of Columbus. The Crump Theater, at over 130 years old, is full of fond memories for generations of residents. The Crump Theater ghost seems to be so fond of the location too, for he has made it his eternal home.

Although the Crump was saved from demolition in the late 1980s, it still needs the community's support to keep it open.

AN INN WITH A STORY

A picturesque setting for a picturesque town, the little town of Story is located twenty minutes south of Nashville, Indiana, on State Road 135 in rural south-central Indiana. The Story Inn isn't just one lone building tucked away in the Indiana landscape...oh no, it is an entire nineteenth century town! Encompassing twelve historic buildings, it is possible to spend the night in an old saw mill, a carriage house, or for the strong-willed — a haunted general store!

The History

Three million acres of central Indiana land was opened up to settlers on September 30, 1809, due to the "10 o'clock Treaty" between Governor William Henry Harrison and the Miami Indian Council. The boundaries were determined on where the shadows were cast on that day, from Raccoon Creek on the Wabash River near Montezuma to Seymour, Indiana. The location where Story, Indiana, now sits is at the boundary of this treaty line, and today a plaque stands next to the old mill house commemorating the treaty.

A medical doctor from southern Ohio, Dr. George Story and his family received a land grant in 1851 from President Millard Fillmore for the tract of land that the Story Inn now stands on. Dr. Story hailed from a hardwood logging family, and was attracted to the area for the generous virgin hardwood forests surrounding the property. The original land grant is on display in the Story Inn for the public to see.

The boom-time for the town of Story was between the years 1880 and 1929, when logging the virgin hardwoods was profitable business. During that time, the town had not one, but two general stores open to local residents and travelers through the area, a nondenominational church, a one-room schoolhouse, a grain mill, a saw mill, a slaughter-house, a permanent blacksmith house (blacksmiths tended to travel around from town-to-town back then), and a post office. When the Great Depression hit in 1929, however, it made economic casualties out of Story and Brown County. Between the years of 1930 and 1940, Brown County saw its population move elsewhere in search of better prospects. Over the course of the decade, eighty percent of the land in Brown County was turned over to the state by farmers who lost their land due to foreclosure. With all the extra land that had been stripped of the forests, the state and national government created the Brown County State Park and Hoosier National Forest. Today these parks boast healthy second growth forests.

An old potbelly stove is a neat artifact from the Story Inn's general store days.

Story limped along through the decades — the remaining general store with its gas pumps supplying most of the trade — as twentieth century progress skipped over the town, preserving the nineteenth century way of life. In the early 1980s, a couple purchased the old general store and began renovating it back into its former glory. They opened up the Story Inn, a four-room bed and breakfast that featured the nineteenth century charm of old Indiana. The bed and breakfast changed hands a few times before the current owner, Rick Hofstetter, purchased the property in 1999. The inn has been transformed into an all-season bed and breakfast, and a gourmet restaurant is managed by popular restaurateur Frank Muller from Indianapolis. The inn still keeps the nineteenth century warmth of its early years...*along with a ghost or two.*

The Haunting

The Blue Lady

With all the buzz about the renovation of buildings from Indiana's past at the Story Inn, it should come as no surprise that there are a few ghosts on the property. The most renowned ghost to call the inn home actually has a guest room dedicated to her — the Blue Lady.

The Blue Lady's true identity and reason for staying in the building even after her death more than a century ago are unknown, however popular belief maintains that she was one of Dr. Story's wives back in the 1800s. The room that is commonly associated with her sits at the top of the staircase of the general store; one of four rooms on the second floor, Hofstetter renamed it in 2001 to the "Blue Lady Room." Yet, the Blue Lady doesn't get her name from the color of her apparition, but rather from a particular blue lamp in her guest room. For this reason, she is sometimes referred to as the "Blue Light Ghost" in older reports. The Blue Lady has been described to wear white or cream colored clothes in the fashion of the 1850s.

She has been sighted numerous times through the years, with reports of her existing *before* the property became a bed and breakfast. For over thirty years now, guests of the old general store have described startling similar accounts of the Blue Lady appearing before them at the foot of the bed, especially if her favorite blue light is lit in the room. The fragrance of cherry tobacco also seems to follow the Blue Lady when she visits patrons of the Story Inn — and in more rooms than just her own. Guests have also been startled to see her stare back at them in the guest room mirror on a few occasions while others staying in the room have walked in to see her standing before the front window, looking out with a melancholy face before fading away. This second report of seeing her apparition looking out the window is backed up by a photo taken in July 2003. The photographer was taking a front-view photo of the old general store. At the time

The front of the Story Inn General Store building... It's been reported that one guest refuses to check out — the Blue Lady.

the building was empty, but clearly in the far left window a face and bust of a woman can be seen looking out the window. She is transparent, but her curious look can be recognized in the picture.

The reason we're able to trace how long reports have been recorded in the bed and breakfast is because every guest room has a guest book for patrons to sign and write about their time there. Rick Hofstetter kept the tradition going after acquiring the property a decade ago and, when reviewing the older books, he was flabbergasted to find consistent accounts about the ghost from former guests. He has a special section of the Story Inn's website dedicated to the haunting. What makes the reports incredible is that each guest book is retired to the attic as soon as it is filled, making it nearly impossible for patrons of the inn to look up older stories. Rick is quick to point out that the accounts before 1997 are more convincing than afterwards because of the Internet spreading the story of his bed and breakfast.

Rick had his own unexplained experience while doing renovations in the closed old general store in 2006. One project was the bathroom in the Blue Lady Room. For three days straight Rick was the last to close up the building and the first to arrive since he lives on the property with his wife — and for three consecutive days, Rick walked in to find water running in the Blue Lady Room. "I am certain that the one valve in question had been turned off each time I locked the building behind me," states Rick. Although he views himself as a skeptic, he has also had other equally unexplained experiences while working at the bed and breakfast.

The Portrait & Other Odd Occurrences

Rick had an interesting experience with an old black and white portrait that hangs above the check-in counter at the Story Inn. The woman in the portrait is unknown, but she sternly stares out at the patrons of the bed and breakfast, dressed in all black with a neatly placed bun of hair pulled behind her head. It seems whenever anyone makes a remark about the appearance of the pictured woman, strange things happen. One time Rick was standing with a friend in front of the old photo when the friend made a negative remark about the pictured woman's appearance. On cue, the photo dropped from where it was hanging high up on the wall and fell face down with perfect comic timing. What stunned Rick was that the picture and its frame had been hanging securely on the hook that he had hung himself. When other similar negative remarks are uttered about the woman in the photo, the cash register has acted up and lights have gone out in the building.

Other employees have their own ghost stories to share about the Inn. Angie Hofstetter, Rick's wife, has worked at the Inn for more than a decade. Sometimes, she reports, you can hear the rustling of long skirts as if some invisible presence was walking around the floor. Others have felt "odd" sensations in the buildings. Angie herself has been pinched on her bottom! The story behind that was that she was working in the kitchen one day rolling out some dough. Suddenly, she was pinched by some unseen force!

Others in the kitchen have had similar experiences to hers. One of the chefs was working in the kitchen one day before the evening dinners arrived. As they worked, the door into the kitchen suddenly burst open and slammed against the wall! After a brief investigation, nothing or no one was found to have caused this...no one visible that is. On another occasion an employee was struck in the hand by a flying

This portrait mysteriously took a nose-dive from its secured hook in front of Rick Hofstetter, the Story Inn's current owner.

plate of spaghetti from the kitchen counter. Again there was no explanation for this...just a mess to clean up afterwards. A different employee was descending the stairs one day when she noticed what looked like a floor-length skirt turn from view at the bottom of the staircase. The skirt was cream in color, but as soon as the employee reached the bottom of the stairs, she could find no one to explain what she had just seen!

The Inn's Many Haunted Places

The team learned some interesting information about the Inn that hadn't been previously mentioned. For example, the "Blue Lady Room" is not the most haunted guest room in the Inn — that dubious honor goes to the Morrison-Kelly Room located down the hall from the Blue Lady Room on the second floor of the general store. Rick has reported high electromagnetic field (EMF) spikes in the bathroom of the Morrison-Kelly Room, in addition to guest book accounts about strange noises heard throughout the night by patrons staying in those quarters.

Another example of stories that have gone largely unknown by most of the public is that the outside buildings — such as the Old Barn, Dr. Story's house, and the Old Mill building — are also active with paranormal experiences, but less so than the General Store building. The team was unable to investigate all of these buildings on this trip, though they did investigate the barn.

Built in 1908, the old barn is one of the rumored paranormal hotspots at the Story Inn.

The Morrison-Kelly guest room is one of the suites available to visitors. It may also be the most haunted room at the Story Inn.

There are marked graves on the Story Inn's property. This headstone, however, was found being used as a counterweight in the barn...no one knows where the grave it belongs to is located.

The Investigation

Because of all the reported haunting at the Story Inn, it has piqued the interest of many paranormal groups, including Hoosier Paranormal Research. On December 27, 2005, the team journeyed to the historic bed and breakfast to conduct an investigation. Members present for this investigation were Kenny, Greg, Shannon, and Robert; they started the evening interviewing the staff and gathering information about their personal experiences at the Story Inn.

Hoosier Paranormal spent the entire night at the Inn, taking photos, conducting EVP sessions, and gathering data. In the course of the evening, they also began to debunk many of the reported noises from the Morrison/Kelly room and phenomena in the Blue Lady Room. The high EMF spikes from the Morrison/Kelly room's bathroom were due to a high power source located on the outside wall of the building. Many of the sounds reported to take place in the room were due to various natural occurrences. The pipes for the sink make sounds when the water is turned on while the floor in the Hendricks guest room bathroom creeks, making it sound like someone is walking up the staircase in the Morrison/Kelly room. In the Blue Lady Room, it was discovered that the mirror is responsible for playing many visual effects on pictures, making it appear as if something paranormal was being photographed. The light anomalies are purely because of the light refraction from the mirror and it could explain why people have seen a woman standing behind them in the mirror when they were alone in the room!

Upon reviewing the data gathered during their investigation, Hoosier Paranormal found four electronic voice phenomena recorded on their equipment and one unexplainable photo. The photo was taken in the Blue Lady Room when one of the investigators, Greg, saw something odd. According to the team's report:

 "[At] 11:27 p.m. Greg sees some sort of red dot on the inside of the door in the Blue Lady Room. He's able to snap a digital picture, which later reveals what we believe to be an Orb. Robert would see the same thing later in this room."

Was it the spirit of the Blue Lady coming in to greet the team? Or perhaps it was someone else? The answer to that question is still inconclusive.

The four EVP clips that the team caught are very interesting, though they're not all fully understood:

Behind the dining area in the General Store building is a flight of wooden stairs to the second floor. Due to age they are a bit uneven, causing a "fun house" effect when climbing them.

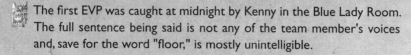

 The first EVP was caught at midnight by Kenny in the Blue Lady Room. The full sentence being said is not any of the team member's voices and, save for the word "floor," is mostly unintelligible.

The second EVP was recorded at 4:34 a.m. in the Morrison/Kelly room by Kenny and Robert. Again, the message is indistinguishable, but it's clearly an anomaly in the recording.

The third EVP is clearly understandable and how it was recorded is quite remarkable. It was caught at 7:51 a.m. in the Blue Lady Room, which had been locked up for the night in order not to disturb the recording equipment in the room. On the recording, you can hear a woman's voice saying "God Bless" in the room...even though no one was in it!

The last EVP was caught several minutes after the last one in the same room, at 8:02 a.m. The room was still locked up to prevent people from coming in, but a female voice is heard saying, "I." Again...there was no explanation for the recording.

Reflections

Different people believe different things about the ghosts of the Story Inn. Its owner Rock Hofstetter has had odd incidents happen to him there, but chalks that up to coincidence. The staff relate to the phenomena differently, giving credit to the ghosts of the old General Store for all the unexplained situations they have found themselves in. Finally, Hoosier Paranormal Research labels the Story Inn as a haunted location, in part because they noted that during their investigation the presence of an invisible spirit could be felt following them.

Hoosier Paranormal also states:

"... based on our evidence, the history, and volume of guest accounts, and employees accounts that the Story Inn is not only haunted by the Blue Lady ghost, but also has a second male spirit that is causing an intelligent haunt."

Is the Story Inn haunted? Perhaps this is a good chance for you — the paranormal enthusiast — to stay the night and discover for yourself!

THE EVER-EERIE
WHISPERS ESTATE

It was a dark and stormy night as I drove up to 714 Warren Street, a gray house covered in vines that looked as if it had just stepped out of a horror movie. Stopping the car to catch a glimpse of my GPS mounted on the dashboard, I looked up to see two stone angels looking at me from across the street. "Ah ha!" I exclaimed to myself. I had found it! I had arrived at the house known as the Whispers Estate...an impressively large Victorian home, nearly reaching 4,000 square feet. The house sits amongst the tree-lined Warren Street where other charming historic homes from the city of Mitchell's past are located. Locals have hushed their voices about Whispers Estate for more than a century since it has such a traumatic and twisted past and, on Halloween night, trick-or-treaters avoid visiting the home during their search for candy. Some locals say unholy things occurred in the house when it was used as a doctor's office while others say it is full of spirits of the dead.

Haunting History

Founded in 1853, the sleepy town of Mitchell has its roots in the American railroad system. The town was originally established around a major railroad company whose tracks ran through south-central Indiana, the Monon Railroad (which was also known as the Chicago, Indianapolis, and Louisville Railway from 1897-1956). During its heyday the Monon Railway served much of Indiana, running lines that connected Chicago, Indianapolis, Michigan City, and Louisville together. Because of this vast network, the trains served the transportation needs of six major Indiana campuses: Indiana University (Bloomington), Purdue University (West Lafayette), Butler University (Indianapolis), Wabash College (Crawfordsville), DePauw University (Greencastle), and St. Joseph's College (Rensselaer).

The university traffic was so important to the Monon Railway that it even painted the passenger cars and engines in the schools' colors; passenger cars were painted red and white for Indiana University and Wabash College and the engines were painted gold and black for Purdue and DePauw universities. Eventually the Monon Railroad merged with the Louisville and Nashville Railroad Company; the tracks are still in use. In 1857, the Ohio and Mississippi Railroad was completed, a railroad that connected Cincinnati, Ohio, to St. Louis, Missouri, and ran right through Mitchell. Because

The ever-eerie Whispers Estate…as many as eight ghosts may reside within its walls.

of all of the industrial transportation running through the town, Mitchell was able to grow and prosper well into the twentieth century.

Mitchell is widely known for being the birthplace of two historic individuals: notorious train robber Sam Bass (1851-1878) and astronaut Gus Grissom (1926-1967). Bass's claim to fame was robbing $60,000 worth of gold from a Union-Pacific Railway train on September 18, 1877 and successively getting away with the loot. To date, this has been the largest sum of money robbed off of the Union-Pacific Railroad. Astronaut Gus Grissom is renowned for being the second American to fly through space while piloting the Mercury-Redstone 4 (aka the Liberty Bell 7). In Spring Mill State Park, just outside of Mitchell, there is a memorial and museum in his Grissom's honor, where the Liberty Bell 7 is displayed along with a number of artifacts from his missions.

Gibbons' Family Secrets

During the heyday of Mitchell, a young man named John Gibbons married his sweetheart Josephine, nicknamed Jessie, on September 10, 1899. John Gibbons had come to the town as a medical student practicing under Mitchell's town doctor. Sometime after the wedding that year, the Gibbons purchased the land now located at 714 Warren Street, which may or may not have already included the large Victorian home since records at that time are sparse. John Gibbons later finished his medical residency and took over the medical practice for the small town from a retiring doctor. The new doctor dedicated part of his large home to his medical practice, opening and advertising his new examination and operating room. Dr. Gibbons operated his business from his home up until a few years before his death in 1944 at the age of 71.

The following years after the practiced opened, the Gibbons family suffered much tragedy. First, the couple lost their only baby girl, Sarah Elizabeth, ten months after her birth to an unknown aliment. Local legends speculate that the Gibbons were hesitant to have children of their own after Sarah Elizabeth's death due to concern that the children would inherit some health or mental issues. However, since the couple loved children, they started to foster orphaned children from around Lawrence County. This is how they purportedly came about fostering a set of twins — Rachel and Ennis — whose mother died at the house after being involved in a carriage accident. Feeling the need to raise the children, the Gibbons welcomed the twins into their home. Stories and local history don't mention how old the twins were when they entered the Gibbons household, but they would live with John and Jessie until their untimely deaths.

The Gibbons Family plot in Mitchell City Cemetery... From left to right: Sarah Elizabeth, Jessie Gibbons, John Gibbons, and a mysterious stone marker.

A Child's Tragic Death

Christmas Day 1912 started as a festive holiday for the Gibbons family. They posed for a family picture while the service staff prepared the home for the day's activities, which included setting up the freshly cut Christmas Tree, placing candles on the branches, and then lighting them. Sometime after the tree had been set up in the front parlor Rachel entered the room. What she was doing in the room is unknown, but it is speculated that she was either sneaking a peek at the neatly wrapped Christmas presents or secretly playing with some of the bottles from her foster father's operating room. An ever-curious eight-year-old, Rachel got too close to the tree and somehow caught her dress on fire. Panicking, she flailed around the room trying to put out the blaze that had quickly spread to the pocket door and wall of the parlor until family members came to her aid to put out the flames. Some speculate that perhaps the fire was accelerated by ether, a common material used in turn-of-the-century operating rooms that is highly flammable. The fire was extinguished, but poor Rachel had severe burns all over her body. Immediately, she was rushed up to her bedroom on the second floor for treatment. For two days, Rachel lay in bed in agony as infection set in and passed away on December 27, 1912.

Although her foster father was a prominent doctor in the area, Dr. Gibbons was unable to stem serious secondary infections, such as gangrene, from infecting Rachel's wounds especially since the antibiotic penicillin had not yet been discovered. Psychics who have visited the home, however, have proposed an alternative theory to explain Rachel's death...one that is more sinister than what the rumors have said. They have proposed that John and Jessie Gibbons, now faced with a deformed child, which they were trying to avoid in the first place by fostering, overdosed Rachel with morphine. The psychics have said that Rachel told them that Dr. Gibbons raised the amount of morphine being fed into her system until her tiny body could no longer tolerate it.

Two years after the death of his twin sister, Ennis passed away in the home. The cause of his death is unknown. Neither of the children were buried in the family gravesite at Mitchell City Cemetery; the only bodies recorded to rest there are Dr. John, his wife Jessie, and baby Sarah Elizabeth (who is marked with a grave marker engraved "S.E."). A fourth grave marker lays next to Dr. John's headstone, but the engraving has long since been worn away by time and the elements. Instead, local legends speak of a number of bodies buried in the backyard of the house. According to Jarret Marshall, a past owner of the home, there are two adults, two children, and a baby buried in the backyard from a discovery made by a team of ghost hunters who had a sonogram. Could this be true? No further investigation has been done to prove or disprove this claim.

This girl in an Edwardian era dress is thought to be Rachel. The photo hangs in the dining room between the pocket and front hallway doors.

The Rest of the Family

Sometime between 1910 and 1920, the Gibbons officially adopted a young girl named Helen. Unlike her ill-fated foster siblings, Helen grew into adulthood with the Gibbons family. She was noted in the 1929 Mitchell High School yearbook a number of times with one photo showing her graceful figure clutching a cello. Not much is known about Helen Gibbons... her last known location was traced to Fort Wayne, Indiana.

Jessie Gibbons died in 1934 of double pneumonia at the age of sixty-one in the upstairs front room, now termed "Jessie's Room." A decade

One of a few photos from the 1929 Mitchell High School yearbook to have Helen Gibbons pictured. Helen is the first person seated in the second row on the left holding a cello.

later, John died of natural causes at the local hospital, and he was laid to rest next to his wife and infant daughter.

Another Tragic Death

After the Gibbons' passed away, the home changed hands and eventually became a tenant house. The home was broken up into individual apartments whose renters shared facilities such as bathrooms, dining area, and the kitchen. It is during this time in the building's history that another death occurred in the home...that of Mr. H's.

I call him "Mr. H" due to the lack of first-hand information about this tragic gentleman. His last name has been reported to be Henderson or Hendelson, and he once rented one of the rooms on the second floor. One day, as he was exiting the tub after bathing, he slipped back into the basin and hit his head on the water faucet, causing him to break his neck. Although his death was swift, the discovery of his body was not — he lay dead in the tub for three days before his body was discovered.

A Home's New Lease

After the accident, the property changed hands a number of times. It was reverted back into a peaceful single-family home with no ghost

The infamous flipping claw foot tub in the second floor bathroom... The water faucets in the sink have also been known to turn on by their own volition.

stories associated with the house, but, according to local stories, the serene life of the house ceased in the early part of the twenty-first century when a young family who lived in the house faced tragedy. The family had a little toddler who was ill with Hydrocephalus (the fancy term for the condition "water-on-the-brain") who fell to his death down the front staircase. The family promptly moved out of the house, which is how it came into the ownership of Jarret Marshall in 2004.

Trained in home restoration, Jarret did not purchase the property with the intent of having a haunted house. In interviews, Jarret claimed to have been attracted to the old property, which he bought on the spot after the inspection results were good. However, as Jarret settled into the home, an increasing amount of odd occurrences began to concern him. Strange things were happing to the point where Jarret couldn't live in the home alone...he started inviting friends and family members to stay the night.

A Paranormal Gem

After several months of haunting occurrences, it was suggested to Jarret that he turn the home into a bed and breakfast in order to have a consistent flow of people staying there. He did this — and the Whispers Estate Bed and Breakfast was created, named after the whispering phantom that Jarret and others would hear while in the house. In 2006, Whispers Estate hit the paranormal community when Jarret requested the services of paranormal investigators after taking a photo that revealed a ghost in the dining room mirror. This has led many paranormal groups to visit the home in hopes of meeting its active spirits...most notably Rachel.

In March 2008, Van Reiner, a paranormal enthusiast, purchased the house from Jarret Marshall. Van had been interested in the house ever since he was there during the Mid-South Paranormal Conference in 2007; he continued to frequently visit the home until purchasing it. Although the house is no longer open as a bed and breakfast, Van runs flashlight tours of the home in addition to allowing paranormal investigative groups to visit nearly every weekend. In May 2009, I met Van at the Indiana Paranormal Conference in Danville, Indiana — and my interest in the home's history was piqued.

News Breaks

Since 2006, Whispers Estate has been featured in numerous documentaries and radio shows regarding the paranormal, in addition to being investigated by various paranormal investigative teams. In 2007, "Children of the Grave," a documentary by the Booth Brothers, filmed their Paranormal Task Force as they investigated the house. Later that year the documentary was aired nationally on the sci-fi channel and caught the attention of even more paranormal investigators. Local newspapers caught wind of the documentary filming at the home and began running their own stories on the Whispers Estate.

In early November 2007, Doug Semig, one of the hosts of "Ghostly Talk," a radio talk show about "all things paranormal," visited the house on the recommendation of fellow ghost enthusiast Shaun Buris. After a bizarre Saturday night in the house, Doug called into the show that Sunday night to talk about his experiences, which were so intriguing that the entire talk show crew — Scott L., Bonnie, and Doug — visited the house December 27, 2007 for the 95th anniversary of Rachel's death.

In 2008, the local Hoosier documentary directed and produced by Dan T. Hall, "Ghost Stories II: Unmasking the Undead," featured an Indiana Ghost Trackers investigation held at the house. Finally, in December 2008, Shaun and Nathan, the hosts of the radio show "The Ghostman and Demonhunter Show," hosted a live broadcast from the estate with Shadows of Indiana, a local paranormal investigative team from the Indianapolis area. All teams, documentaries, and broadcasts were able to capture more than one unexplained phenomenon while recording in the house!

Happy Spectral Family

For being over a century old, the Whispers Estate has accumulated a plethora of supernatural residents that are said to haunt the home. Many visitors to the house have remarked on its haunting, even if they weren't looking for it. Paranormal personalities have claimed the house to be the most haunted location they've been to...even more active than the notorious Waverly Hills Sanatorium or the *USS Queen Mary*. With disembodied voices that answer questions as soon as you ask them, the Whispers Estate has earned the tag line, "Where even the walls can talk."

From what I could count, there are eight — *yes, eight* — active ghosts said to reside within the walls of the Whispers Estate. That means for every 411-square feet of space in the house there is a ghost to occupy it...that's a ghost per room! The eight reported ghosts are: the Old Hag, Rachel, Ennis, Jessie Gibbons, Mr. H, the baby, Dr. Gibbons, and Big Black. Each spirit listed has their own special place in the house except for two; Rachel and Big Black have been reportedly seen on multiple floors.

There are so many accounts of activity in this house that I can't just group it up in the usual "personal experiences" and "investigations" sub-chapters that have been used in different articles in this book. Instead, each room in the house has been given a special sub-chapter in which the resident ghost and personal experiences are introduced. There are so many eye-witness accounts from this home that I can't possibly fit them all into one chapter, however I do my best to include the most frequently recorded phenomena as well as stories from select paranormal investigators, radio shows, and my own accounts while visiting the home in June and August of 2009.

Search the Internet and you'll find it littered with personal experiences with the paranormal from the Whispers Estate. In fact, on my first visit to the house in June 2009, there was a trio of young professionals visiting the house just for that purpose...to have their own personal experience with a ghost. Lilo, Stitch, and Whachamahibit, as they have requested to be called, had read the stories about Whispers Estate on the Internet and thought it would be a swell idea to test them out. They weren't paranormal investigators; they were just interested in seeing what would happen there. In the end, the trio didn't run into anything overtly paranormal that weekend, but it was interesting meeting curious individuals who were not in the paranormal community and hearing what they had to say about the reported phenomena at Whispers Estate.

A lot does happen in the house... The first investigators to look into the strange phenomena was the Indiana Ghost Trackers, which Lisa Bradley was a member of back in 2006. When asked about the case, she remarked, "This is one of the most well documented houses I've ever been to." When the team first met with Jarret Marshall about the possible haunting of the home, he gave them a stack of papers about an inch thick full of facts about the home and his experiences. "No other homeowner has been that prepared," Lisa noted.

Mayhem in the Attic

The attic plays host to two mischievous yet chilling ghosts at Whispers Estate: Big Black and the Old Hag. When Jarret purchased the home, the attic was unfinished — in fact the entire house was in horrible condition. Seeing a chance to create his own personal space in the house, he began to fix up and finish the attic with the help of friends. One of the new additions to the attic was a permanent wooden staircase that replaced the only access to the attic, a pull down ladder from the ceiling. Another addition to the attic were mirrors, particularly in a small room known as the séance room.

It seems, though, that when Jarret began his renovations in the attic, he provoked the "Old Hag." It isn't known for sure who she was in life, but there are two hypotheses: the first is that the Old Hag was the nanny for the Gibbons home; the other is that the Old Hag was a mentally unstable relative of Jessie Gibbons. It has been conjectured that the Gibbons were reluctant to have children of their own because of the threat of the child inheriting a mental problem, perhaps the same one that the Old Hag suffered from, such as schizophrenia. During the turn-of-the-century it was seen as a stigma to the family to have a handicapped family member and that was something the upstanding Gibbons would abhor.

Odd occurrences started as soon as work begun in the attic and have continued to this day. According to one interview, Jarret and some friends

The attic is a hotspot for paranormal activity in the house.

This room is known as the séance or "voodoo" room at the Whispers Estate. The ghost **Big Black** is known to lurk here as well as on the first floor of the home. Contrary to its name, the room was never used for either spiritual or voodoo rituals.

were sitting on the stairs that led up to the attic when the apparition of the Old Hag came screaming at them! Spooked, the entire group went running from the stairwell. Once most of the renovations were finished, Jarret was only able to sleep in his new room for three nights before nightmares drove him to sleep elsewhere in the house. As of today the attic is still unfinished, and Van has also reported having many night terrors while sleeping in the room. In addition to the nightmares, guests or investigators often feel "pins and needles" all over their limbs as they enter the room, described to be the same sensation one feels when a limb has fallen asleep.

Another spooky story about the attic was told to me by Amanda F., whose husband John has helped to fix up the house. She said that John was working up in the attic one day and heard what could be described as phantom hammering working alongside him. John could hear the sound of the hammer and feel the vibration as if a hammer was being pounded on the floor in front of him. In another account, John asked for one of the ghosts to flick his hat off his head during an EVP session...a few minutes later the ghosts obliged by throwing his hat across the room.

Psychics have also reported that the attic has the feeling of "death and rebirth," since it is the end of a vortex that extends throughout the house. Passersby have claimed to see a woman dressed in white, looking out the third floor window at the world outside.

When the "Ghostly Talk" radio crew visited the home in December 2007, members took turns sitting with Jarret up in the attic to participate in one-on-one EVP sessions. Shortly before Doug and Jarret went up to the attic, Doug had asked for a jumping jack's ball from Rachel since none had been found with the game set in her room. While the pair sat in the dark attic recording their EVP session, there was a thumping noise shortly before Jarret was hit in the head by a piece of plywood. After the commotion, Doug found a small ball sitting behind him lying on the floor of the attic.

The next investigator to join Jarret up in the attic was Bonnie. The pair, in an attempt to get a response from Rachel, sang "Ring Around the Rosie," but in the middle of the song Bonnie was hit by a another ball. On the recording you can hear a ball bouncing around the room, however when they looked for the ball, they couldn't find it. An odd thing happened, though — *nine new jacks* appeared on the floor around them. After the group finished up their investigation for the night, Bonnie went to bed upstairs in the attic. She was woken up during the night by a heavy sensation of someone sitting at the foot of her bed. She felt that if she moved her feet, she would hit whoever was there, but no one was visibly present. Exhausted, Bonnie rolled over and went back to sleep, ignoring whatever — *or whoever* —was seeking her attention.

Located above the kitchen is the old service quarters for hired help. Rachel has been known to play with toy balls in the room.

Scary Service Quarters

The service quarters are located in the back of the second floor and is basically one large, very yellow, un-insulated room. The room once was the quarters for the Gibbons' hired help, and there is a back stairwell that leads down into the kitchen located in the back of the room. Jarret had partially finished this back room to use as his private quarters as well, but this never came to pass. The back room isn't immune to unexplained occurrences either. Paranormal investigators have reported feeling a strange and uneasy atmosphere while in the room.

EMF detectors have spiked in one particular back corner of the room when being carried by one or two people...only to suddenly drop off when more people notice the phenomena occurring. Toy balls have been said to roll around the floor on their own volition and there have been sightings of Rachel's figure roaming from the upstairs hallway into the service closet located next to the stairwell. The sounds of children running on the back stairs can be heard from time to time in the house; they are believed to be Rachel and possibly Ennis.

Bathroom with a Boo

The second floor bathroom is the scene of Mr. H's accidental death. Since then, strange things have occurred in there, especially in the first few years that Jarret owned and restored the house. When Jarret purchased the house, the bathtub was one of the only things left in the large home. No one knows if the tub is original or not, or even the one Mr. H reportedly died in, but on one occasion it mysteriously flipped onto its side. It took five men for the tub to be straightened back to its original position, and then a few plumbers to fix the pipes that burst during the event. It is a heavy tub, and no explanation has been given as to how it could flip by itself, especially since no one saw it happen. The sink faucets also have been known to turn on by themselves and a foul stench of decay has been detected coming from the room. Much of the strange activity has decreased over the years since Jarret unearthed the story about Mr. H's accidental death.

Rachel's Room

Rachel is by far is the most well-known ghost at Whispers Estate. Her story is the most detailed and probably the most frequently told out of all the others who have died in the home. Most guests to the house will ask to see Rachel while on ghost hunts or investigations. Rachel seems to be more interactive with the public than the other alleged ghosts, with quite a few videos on "You Tube" and photos circulating around the Internet claiming to be images or sounds of her. In fact the photo that made Whispers Estate the mecca of paranormal phenomena in Indiana

Rachel is rumored to have passed away in this room... Today guests leave toys and dolls in the room for her to play with.

was a photo of Rachel being reflected in a mirror in the dining room. EVPs have been recorded of Rachel talking, running, and singing in the house...something I even *experienced* for myself.

One of the most sought after recordings by paranormal investigators and ghost hunters alike is of Rachel walking in the second floor hallway. According to Van, she has frequently been seen roaming the second floor between 10:15 and 10:45 p.m. He pointed out that if guests to the house manage to set up in Jessie's room by 10:05 p.m., chances are good that you may see Rachel's form walk through the hallway. This phenomenon has been documented in a segment of Dan Hall's documentary "Ghost Stories II: Unmasking the Dead," during which members of Indiana Ghost Trackers saw a small form of a girl roaming the hallway and then darting back into the service quarters. It was as if she was curious about the investigators, but too shy to greet them. Although Dan and Van were present in the room with the investigators at the time, they failed to see the apparition from their vantage point.

Rachel's presence has also been detected in her old bedroom. Guests have heard both Rachel's painful screams of agony and children's laughter originating from this room while visiting. Psychics have reported various occurrences; one got a sense of duality in the room especially around the bed; the other interacted with her ghost. According to the first psychic, the left side of the bed has positive energy flowing through it while the right side of the bed has negative energy. Guests who have slept on the left side of the bed have reported sleeping perfectly fine through the night while those who slept on the right side had horrible nightmares. It has been speculated that this duality reflects Rachel's life: her happy times with the Gibbons and her agonizing death. A second psychic reported meeting Rachel's spirit, during which Rachel attempted to pull the psychic into the afterlife to be her new "mommy."

A group of paranormal investigators who visited the house last year had an eerie experience involving a coloring book. The group had laid out the coloring book and a box of crayons on the floor of Rachel's Room so Rachel could color. Before the group opened the crayon box, they left the room to gather some extra equipment. Van stood in the doorway of the room watching them walk down the front stairs. The group returned to find that the crayon box had been opened and a few strokes colored into the book! Van swears that he did not touch the coloring book or crayons, and no one had gone in the room while he stood watch at the door.

Guests who have slept in the room have experienced the phenomena: some have reported waking up to find a child standing next to the bed watching them, being woken up by some invisible child jumping or sitting on the bed, or having their hair stroked while laying in bed. Whispers and murmuring have also been heard in the room, even when all the guests are accounted for. I visited the house in August 2009 with friend

Lisa Bradley and, while in the middle of an EVP session, Lisa and Van claimed to have seen a white silhouette run by the room's door.

Jessie's Room

The front room on the second floor is named for Jessie Gibbons, who passed away in that room in 1934 after fighting double pneumonia for two weeks. Their ten-month old daughter Sarah Elizabeth also died in this room of unknown causes. Guests who have spent the night in that room have reported hearing labored breathing and the smell of baby powder floating through the air.

Ennis, Rachel's twin brother, also is said to haunt the closet in the room. Guests have *heard* and *seen* the doorknob jiggle before the door pops open. The funny thing is that this door doesn't easily open — the handle needs to be physically pressed down in order to release the bolt. According to a paranormal group that investigated the house in September 2009, they distinctly heard the voice of Jessie Gibbons telling them she preferred the closet door to be open. Psychics have also stated seeing Jessie's apparition looking out the window for her husband, possibly knowing he was out visiting one of his rumored mistresses.

A fun fact for movie buffs is that the bed in Jessie's Room is a prop from the movie "Interview with a Vampire." It was used in the scene where Brad Pitt is kissed by a young Kirsten Dunst, and because of this, the room is the most requested room in the house to sleep in. Jarret came to own the famous bed frame as a thank you gift from homeowners who appreciated his work on their house down in New Orleans. It is an antique, so take care when getting on and off of the bed, as it has been damaged by previous guests.

A Haunted Hallway & Spooky Stairs

If the front staircase could talk, it would have some interesting stories to tell, especially since it is rumored to have had a death occur on it. Amanda told me about one of her experiences while investigating the house with her team, SHADOWS of Indiana. She said the group was in the first floor parlor when they could hear the distinct sounds of a child running up the staircase. When the team walked over to investigate, they found a small foot print left in the dust from the drywall being installed earlier that day. The team took a photo — and it clearly shows the impression of a child's foot. What is odd about the foot print is that although the entire staircase was covered in dust, the only step to have a footprint was the one in the middle of the staircase. In addition the entire team was wearing shoes and no children were present in the house.

A similar account told to me was about a ghost hunter who saw a leg on the staircase landing. According to the story, a team was cleaning up their

Eerie phenomenon occurs in this room, including sounds of labored breathing and a closest door popping open. The figure of Jessie has been seen standing by the front window.

This spooky stairwell is the play area for spectral children.

equipment after investigating the house one weekend. One of the members, Shaun, was coiling up the extension cords up the stairwell when he noticed a child's shoe and white stocking step down onto the landing without making a sound. Startled, the investigator stumbled back a few steps before looking for the rest of the phantom child, who had disappeared.

There is also an account of a doll being thrown down the staircase by an invisible force during the time Jarret lived in the house. If you visit the home, sitting on the chest of drawers in Rachel's Room is a small plastic doll with red hair that has been horribly burned and disfigured. According to the story, a friend of Jarret's brought that doll to the house as a gift to Rachel, but it disappeared from the house soon after it was "given" to her. A few years later, the doll resurfaced when that same friend of Jarret's inquired about where it was. A minute after the friend asked, the doll was thrown down the main staircase towards Jarret and his friend, but it didn't look anything like how it originally did. The doll had become disfigured, and parts of it have been melted and burned. Its plastic hair had been scorched in places and pulled out at others. Van showed me the doll on my first visit and explained that its condition has continued to worsen — it looks like it is more burnt now than how it was when it was originally thrown down the stairwell (there are pictures of the doll from that day). Van did point out that the added wear could be from many different people handling the little plastic doll, but that still doesn't explain how the doll became burnt in the first place.

On my most recent visit to the house in August 2009, I slept in the parlor with my husband Mike since the air-conditioning unit was not pushing cool air to the second or third floors. I woke up multiple times during the night to the sounds of children playing on the stairs and in the front hallway. The first time I woke up, I could clearly hear the sound of a child running up and down the hallway between the front door and the dining room...the sound of hard soled shoes was the most distinct to me. As soon as I piped up a "who's there?" the sound stopped. An hour later, I woke up to a door slamming on the second floor; a few minutes after that I could hear someone running up the front stairwell, yet again wearing hard-soled shoes. What was peculiar about the sound of going up the stairs is that it just stopped as soon as it hit the middle of the stairwell. The next morning I searched around the second and third floors looking for an explanation for the sounds I heard, but I failed to find one.

Whispers in the Operating Room

Dr. Gibbons still roves around his old home watching all that goes on there, or at least it seems like he does. The ghosts of Whispers Estate start to become active around 10 o'clock at night, and it is the fragrance of Dr. Gibbons' aftershave or old cigars that heralds the arrival. In many accounts, the odor of Dr. Gibbons' aftershave has been detected in the

Sounds of "cooing" or "kissing" have been heard by female visitors to the house who enter the Operating Room alone.

parlor room, dining room, and even the operating room before the sounds of running can be heard overhead or a deep growl from below.

Today Dr. Gibbons' examination and operating rooms have been transformed into a spacious guest suite, but back when the doctor still owned the land it was the scene of many gruesome events. It is said that Rachel and Ennis's mother died in that room, possibly along with count-less other individuals. Investigators who have done EVP sessions in the room have reported hearing women's voices saying "Help me" or "Save me" upon playback on their audio recorders.

Unexplainable *earthquakes* have also been reported to occur in the bathroom in the suite on more than one occasion while others have seen and felt the bed in the room shake, as if something was thumping on the bed while investigators were sitting on it. Women tend to be the victims of many unexplained phenomena in the room, reporting hearing kiss-ing or cooing noises in their ear, whispers, and on some accounts, being groped or touched on parts of their bodies. Some psychics who have walked through the house have reported that Dr. Gibbons was a voyeur, womanizer, and kept many mistresses around town.

The newest entity to be experienced in the home, Big Black, is speculated to have arrived when Jarret purchased an old church pew to

Shortly after Jarrett purchased this old church pew the phantom known as Big Black made his appearance. Is the pew cursed or is it just a coincidence?

use in the house. The phantom has been described to be six to eight feet tall, pitch black, and seems to absorb light while appearing suddenly to investigators. He was first reportedly seen in the doctor's operating room, which led visitors to guess that he was somehow related to the old medical practice. Others speculate that perhaps Big Black is an elemental, a type of inhuman entity that is attuned to or composed of the major elements of the earth (fire, soil, water, and air) and can hold positive or negative intentions. Some people think of him as a protector of the home rather than a negative influence, but rumor spread that it was Big Black who forced Jarret to quickly flee from the home.

For only being open to the public for less than five years, there is a plethora of experiences reported to come out of Whispers Estate. One of the experiences Van reported to me was about John from SHADOWS of Indiana and it is the same story John's wife also told me. Amanda and John had visited the house many times since June 2007 with their paranormal group and became friends with both Jarret and Van. According to the account, John, Amanda, Van, and Jarret had been working in the house for awhile when they decided to take a break one afternoon. While John used the first floor Operating Room Suite bathroom, the other three stood around the dining room chit-chatting until John walked out of the suite...

Visitors to the Whispers House have reported feeling this bathroom shake. There have also been **EVPs** of pleas for help by ghostly patients recorded.

pale white and in shock. After regaining his composer, he asked if anyone else had felt the massive earthquake. The trio looked at each other and shook their heads. Now discovering they had a mystery on their hands, they asked John to explain. John said that while using the bathroom he experienced a violent earthquake, so violent that he thought the house was about to come down on top of them all. However, it was only contained to that single room because Amanda, Van, and Jarret — who had been standing right outside of the suite — never felt a thing.

The same phenomenon was experienced again three weeks later, this time by a couple who was visiting the house on a ghost hunt. According to Van, who was leading a tour of the house, a woman had to use the restroom and, knowing the stories about the Operating Room's groping ghost, brought her husband along to stand guard in the bathroom. Van had been talking in the parlor and hadn't reached the stories about the suite's bathroom yet when the couple came shooting out of the suite...pale and shaking. The pair said they had been in the bathroom when, again, the whole room violently shook. They said it was like a 6.0 magnitude earthquake was hitting southern Indiana...yet the rest of the group hadn't felt a thing.

Another account of paranormal play in the Operating Room comes from Van about members of Indiana Ghost Trackers Indianapolis Chapter. While the group was conducting an EVP session in the suite, the bed suddenly started to shake violently...as if a miniature earthquake was occurring. Although it was dim in the room, members who were sitting on the bed could see a clipboard and papers shaking with the vibrations of the "earthquake." When the team left the room, they quickly told Van about their experience. Another incident that happened to the group, according to Van, was that a male member of the IGT-Indianapolis was in the Operating Room during the EVP session when he clearly felt a drop of water drip onto the back of his neck. When he felt around for the drop, he couldn't find it. The member called this phenomena "spirit water," because although the sensation of water dripping is definitely felt, physically there isn't any evidence left behind.

Dining with the Dead

The dining room is at the heart of the entire home, and although activity in the room is rare, it still occurs. Guests of the home have reported seeing shadowy children playing peek-a-boo under the table as they sit in the parlor at night. Adorning the walls of the dining room is a large mirror and series of old photos or paintings that Van or Jarret have picked up through the years from antique stores or estate sales. One old photo located between the parlor's pocket door and the entrance to the room from the entryway depicts a young girl in an Edwardian era frilly white dress, black boots and leggings, and a large white head bow. Van believes this to be a photo of Rachel. Across the room is a large mirror...

this is where Jarret caught a photo of a small ghost girl also believed to be Rachel.

Van recounted for me two stories about people witnessing apparitions walking through the dining room; one was about a friend visiting the home while the other was a story from a lawn service worker. In his first story, Van said that one of his female friends was visiting the house one evening and had the fright of her life. While sitting at the dining room table on the chair closest to the kitchen talking to Van, she happened to look up in time to watch the transparent apparition of a small girl (thought to be Rachel) descending the staircase from the second floor. The woman quickly stood up and backed up against the wall away from the table in time to watch Rachel cross into the dining room and sit in the vary chair the woman had just been sitting on. Then the apparition just dissolved into the air shortly after sitting down... The other story Van recounted was a personal experience from a gentleman hired to take care of the lawn. One spring day, just after Van had purchased the property, the gentleman was mowing the lawn and happened to pass the large windows that look into the dining room. Knowing that Van was out of the house and that no one was visiting, the gentleman didn't expect to see anything strange while glimpsing at the windows, but he did — he saw a tall shadowy figure walk from the front hallway towards the doctor's examination room. Shaken at what he had seen, the gentleman stopped working and left immediately.

Whispers Estate has received its name from the many occurrences of unexplainable whispers, murmurs, and disembodied voices encountered in the house. Jarret originally named the house from his experiences, but Van also has his own story about disembodied voices. One day while he was working in the back bathroom shortly after he purchased the home, he could clearly hear two women talking in a conversation in the dining room. Thinking it was two of his friends who had arrived unannounced for a visit, Van got up to greet them. Reaching the threshold of the dining room, he quickly realized that no one else was in the house with him. Perplexed, Van returned to work in the back bathroom.

The stories of whispers in the dining room don't end with just Van's account — Lisa Bradley also has experienced the phenomena, albeit in a more belated fashion. On my second trip to the house, I had invited Lisa to join my husband, Van, and myself for a night of poking around. For the first hour that we were at the home, the four of us sat around the dining room table just talking about whatever was on our minds, all the while recording the conversation on the hunch that one of the ghosts may attempt to join in — and Rachel did just that. My recorder failed to record anything out of the ordinary that night, but Lisa's managed catch what we think to be Rachel saying some phrases to us. One EVP Lisa caught may be Rachel saying, "You

The walls really do talk... The parlor is an area where houseguests frequently hear disembodied voices speaking to them.

said Lisa," and at another point in our conversation we can hear someone humming a melody...but it wasn't any of us in the room.

Poignant Parlor

The front parlor seems to be a central location in the house for haunted activity. It is in this room that many have heard the moans and wails of Rachel, children inexplicably laughing, loud sounds of furniture being dragged, and the cries of the Old Hag and baby. Those who have sat or slept on the couch have reported tremors from the floor or the feeling of being rocked while sleeping.

The parlor is the only place in the house where you frequently get audible responses back, according to Van. He pointed out that on the Internet there are several videos posted recording the disembodied voices that can be heard in the parlor. He also noted that the most recent disembodied voice he heard was in February of 2009...it was an unnerving scream and wail from the second floor thought to be Rachel crying out in pain. Other disembodied voices reportedly heard in the parlor are a baby crying, the Old Hag's cackle, and Dr. Gibbons' growl.

Psychics have noted that the parlor seems to be the starting point for a vortex that spans throughout the house. They have also noted that more spirits seem to enter and exit the house at that point in the parlor than the ghosts that reside in the home. Perhaps this is why many of the horizontal beams in the house (such as door thresholds and the fireplace mantels) have registered higher EMF readings.

The Skeptics

For all the talk of how much activity Whispers Estate has going on within its walls, there is an equal amount of talk about how the home's haunting is all bunk. In fact, some of the home's past owners and tenants have stated that they never ran into any ghost or goblins while living in the house until reports surfaced in 2006. Much of the history of the house is unknown, such as who built it in the first place and when. Pieces of local lore about Whispers Estate don't collaborate with the known history of the property, such as Rachel and Ennis' complete existence. In the end, it leaves researchers scratching their heads on what is fact and what is fiction about this house.

The first wall researchers run into is the lack of proof that Rachel or Ennis ever lived in the house, since there are no records that can be found to substantiate that the twins lived with the Gibbons. The census records between 1900 and 1910 taken in Mitchell show no children living with the family, although it could be possible that Rachel and Ennis lived and died in the years between when the census was taken. Local lore does not tell us how long Rachel and Ennis lived with the Gibbons, and we can only guess really how old the twins were when they passed away. To compound the mystery, there are no birth or death records from that time period in Mitchell accounting for Rachel or Ennis. So we're stuck questioning if they ever lived at all.

Van has continued to look for bits of Whispers Estate history in official and unofficial records of the time, but has found few facts to clear up some of the questions about the home's history. However, he has managed to

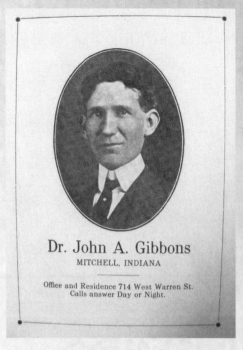

Dr. John A. Gibbons

MITCHELL, INDIANA

Office and Residence 714 West Warren St.
Calls answer Day or Night.

Dr. John Gibbons, as he appeared in the 1916 Mitchell High School yearbook. The photo was used in combination with an ad for his medical services and office located inside the house.

accumulate some old yearbooks that prove that Dr. Gibbons did indeed live and practice out of his house on 714 Warren Street. There are also photos from the 1929 yearbook of Helen Gibbons, proving she was with the family, but documents about the property's history are few and far between.

In one interview, Jarret said he had found records of the fire in the local newspaper, but when he went back to the library to print off the articles, they had been removed from the library's archives. Jarret believes there is someone out there who doesn't want the history of the Whispers Estate told...

Reflections

The stories and accounts about the Whispers Estate fascinate me. Some read like accounts from a horror movie while others remind us of more pleasant times in Indiana's history. While I was visiting the house, Van and I talked in great length about the types of haunting occurring there. Are they residual hauntings or intelligent ones? Could they possibly be a mix of the two? It certainly seems that way to me after the many stories I collected from guests who have visited the house over the recent years. Some occurrences, such as Rachel walking in the second floor hallway between 10:15 and 10:45 p.m., fit the description of a *residual* haunting...however having Rachel actually interact with the paranormal investigators looking for her during that time is a mark of an *intelligent* haunting.

Do I believe Whispers Estate to be haunted? Yes...but not in the sensational way others tend to portray the property. In my limited time visiting the house, I never experienced anything in real time that I can conclusively attribute to the paranormal. Sure I heard what sounded like kids playing up and down the front stairs, but I was also half asleep when I heard it. However, I also collected a few EVPs while conducting

It is speculated that five graves are in the backyard of the Whispers House, two of which are believed to be Rachel and Ennis.

interviews in the house and, since multiple people have heard the same thing in them that I have *(even my exceedingly skeptical husband)*, I have concluded that something ghostly really does roam the halls of the Whispers Estate.

Are there really eight ghosts roaming around the place? Probably not...at least not of the intelligent type. There seem to be only three actual ghosts residing at Whispers Estate: Rachel, her foster father Dr. Gibbons, and the entity known as Big Black. Out of all the stories I heard about the house, only these three have actually interacted with those visiting the home. The wailing, crying, cackling, and sounds of children running coming from the second floor are probably purely residual.

It has been said time and time again: the ghosts of Whispers Estate have never harmed a person visiting the house. Van and Jarret have both said in interviews that they have never felt threatened while living in the home, just startled at times. During the day, the house feels as welcoming and friendly as any other home, but at night the atmosphere changes as the ghosts get ready to appear. There seems to be a theme of duality at the Whispers Estate: happy and sad times, life and death, the living and the dead...they all converge here in, of all places, Mitchell, Indiana.

3

THE INVESTIGATIONS & PERSONAL EXPERIENCES

GOING GHOST HUNTING

Whispers in Raintree

Picturesquely sitting along North Bryan Avenue is a beautiful old red-brick building known as the Raintree House. The Organization of American Historians (OAH) now calls the old structure home — and so does a century-old ghost! The property has seen its share of important events through Bloomington and Indiana University's past, being that it was established a mere twenty-seven years after Bloomington became a city.

The History

The residence known as the Raintree House was built in 1845 and was originally called the Millien House by its first owners. Built out of locally produced redbrick and virgin walnut timber, this grand home caught the attention of the Bloomington public. From 1882 to 1925, the house was run and occupied by the prestigious Rogers family of Bloomington. The home changed hands and names in 1925, becoming the Wellswood House after Agnes Wells, the Dean for Women, purchased the estate. Agnes Wells occupied the home until 1944. Geneva L. Graeba then purchased the property, but she only lived there two years before it was purchased by Indiana University to be rented out to students and personnel of the university between 1946 and 1949.

Wellswood House once again became a private residence when Anna and Newton Stallknecht purchased the property in 1949. They renovated the house and restored the interior back into the home's former splendor, in addition to adding an elaborate garden to the property. The couple also renamed the property Stallknect House once the work was done, and continued to live in the home for the next twenty years. Eventually Indiana University once again purchased the property, this time intending to move the Indiana University Foundation Office into the building. The name "Raintree House" was given to the old home in 1969 by the university, but the Indiana University Foundation would not relocate there, so instead the Organization of American Historians moved into the house in 1970. This is due to an agreement between Herman B. Wells and the chairmen of the OAH at the time, when the office was looking for a new residence.

Raintree House was added to the National Register of Historic Places on September 29, 2004. It joins many other landmarks around the university of having such an honor, including the Student Building, Maxwell Hall, Owen Hall, and other buildings set in the Old Crescent section of campus.

The Legends

Now over 160 years old, many strange and unexplained phenomena are rumored to happen on the Raintree House's property. According to members of OAH who work in the building daily, unexplainable scents, such as the smell of roses, or incredibly strong and indescribable odors have wafted through the house on occasion. Strange noises have been reportedly heard at night by staffers, who have also seen unidentified shapes run through their peripheral vision.

Local legend holds that the home used to be a stop on the Underground Railroad before and during the Civil War. The Raintree House played host to escaping slaves from the southern states, holding them in the basement or the attic until it was safe for them to escape under the cloak of night. Emotions ran high during this period of America's history, and the residents of Bloomington were not spared. Naturally, due to the sensitive nature of the subject matter, no records have ever been found to indicate such a rumor was true.

Another legend coming out of Raintree House tells the story of a tragic washerwoman who worked in the home around the 1850s. According to the legend, the washerwoman was busily working in the basement of the home around a vat of lye soap. For those who are not familiar with lye or lye soap, it is a corrosive alkaline substance. Lye is also known as sodium hydroxide or Caustic Soda and had many household uses in the nineteenth century, from food preservation to cleaning solvents. In this case, the washerwoman was using a strong combination of lye in the soap to clean the laundry of the residents of the home. This unfortunate woman was steadily working away in the basement around the vat of lye soap when she accidently tripped — falling into the vat! The corrosiveness immediately went to work on her skin, causing chemical burns wherever it touched. In alarm, the woman screamed, swallowing a lethal amount of lye soap in the process. She is believed to have died in the basement shortly after falling in and, to this day, the washerwoman is said to haunt the basement... over a century after her death!

The Investigation

It was a clear and quiet night in May 2008 as members of Indiana Ghost Trackers Bloomington and Terre Haute approached the old Raintree House. The fifteen-member group was set to visit the premises on a ghost hunt to see if they could either disprove or capture the paranormal activity reported there. After a brief tour of the location, along with hearing some of the stories of unexplained phenomena, the team split into two small groups to investigate and gather data from the home. For two and a half hours the group gathered data, using digital and video cameras, digital audio recorders, cell sensors, and K2 meters to measure electromagnetic fluctuations. Every half hour the groups of investigators rotated through the house to take photos and do EVP sessions.

During one of the rotations, an IGT-Bloomington member, J.E., took a photo in a ground floor office. What made this photo special is that it shows an unexplained pink, wavy, and transparent anomaly that seems to fade as it trails to the left side of the picture, suggesting that something was in motion when the photo was snapped. Although the other members of the group examined the photo after the investigation, no explanation as to how such an anomaly was created could be found.

During the course of the ghost hunt, team members reported hearing a faint conversation being held in one of the side rooms on the first floor. After investigating where the conversation originated,

Could this photo contain the ghostly face of the phantom washerwoman in the basement of Raintree House?

An anomaly is discovered in the photographs taken at the Raintree House. Is this evidence of ghostly phenomenon?

it was concluded that the conversation was *not* being held between the living visitors of the Raintree House. The basement was also the location of another interesting photograph taken during the ghost hunt. One of the team members took a photo of the basement room next to the water heater and, after examining it, a light orange anomaly was discovered sweeping in front of the water heater and basement wall. Some people who look at the photo claim they see a face while others see a sleeve.

EVPs Collected

"It is always possible that hunt members can speak out of turn in whispered voices, unnoticed by other members, and unable to recall later," says Melanie Hunter, the PR Director of Indiana Ghost Trackers Bloomington.

Melanie added, though, that all IGT investigators are trained in collecting data for investigations and that one of the points they are constantly reminded not to do is whisper during an EVP session. IGT members are trained to note every outside noise that could be misinterpreted as an EVP, including cars, planes, or other external noises.

Numerous EVPs were caught during their investigation that night:

 The first EVP was recorded on the first floor of the home, near the basement stairwell. Melanie's group had been chatting amongst themselves before sitting down to do a formal EVP session, a common practice for the group. Some members believe that ghosts respond to casual chatter just as well as in formal EVP question sessions. During this casual chatter time, the phrase "Basement…basement door" was recorded on Melanie's digital audio device. The voice wasn't heard by anyone on the team at the time it was recorded, and its pitch doesn't match anyone in the group that night.

 The second EVP recorded was also caught on the first floor, this time in an office. In this particular incident, the group was discussing the air conditioning in that particular room when, on Melanie's digital voice recorder, came the phrase "No, I have no idea when that was…" Again, Melanie cannot explain the phrase on the recording. It doesn't match any of the members' voices investigating the room, nor does it make sense with their conversation.

 The third and final EVP caught during the Raintree House visit was recorded in the basement. The EVP seems to be in response to a question posed to any ghost present in the basement with the team: "Is anyone here enjoying our conversation?" A few seconds after that question was asked a faint response is recorded, "yeah." It was not audible to the team members at the time, but it's clearly present on the digital recording. Maybe this was the ghost of the poor washerwoman, grateful for some company that recognized her.

Reflections

After reviewing this case, it seems that there are both residual spirits and an intelligent one roaming the halls of the Raintree House in the later hours of the night. It could be that the residual spirits are just the remnants of more traumatic emotions that have somehow been recorded into the environment. Some paranormal enthusiasts and investigators believe that if emotions run high enough, they can be imprinted into a setting. Since the house is said to have been a stop on the Underground Railroad, it could be the emotions felt by those escaping the South that have been embedded into the house's surroundings. Whatever is haunting the Raintree House, though, is pure speculation without future investigations and further data to examine.

In the end, this home has seen its share of changes: from Millien House, to Wellswood House, to Stallknect House, to finally the Raintree House…it seems to change names with each owner of the property. For over 160 years, this red-brick home has been a steady landmark of the city, having played silent watcher to Bloomington's progress almost since the city was founded. Indiana University has kept the home in great shape, and the staff at the Organization of American Historians seem to really love the place. Indiana Ghost Trackers feels honored to have had the privilege to visit such an important location and believes that if any spirits reside within Raintree's walls...they are neutral observers of our modern times.

Spooks, Smells, & Odd Sensations

Ghost Hunting with IGT Bloomington

It was a warm April night as the members Indiana Ghost Trackers Bloomington gathered in a remote cemetery rumored to abound with activity. One of the chapter members, Bill, had arranged the "ghost hunt" that night, which focused on the old rural graveyard "Cemetery X." Although cemeteries are rarely places that seasoned investigative teams such as IGT Bloomington visit, the ghostly activity and apparitions sighted in the old cemetery piqued the chapter's interest — and we truly had an interesting night there....

One of the wonderful characteristics of the Indiana Ghost Trackers organization that I love is that the group allows members of the public who are interested in ghost hunting the chance to actually experience a true ghost hunt before joining. Many of the current members throughout the state have entered into the group this way, and this night was no different. We had fourteen people in total during our visit: Lisa, the Chapter and Regional Director; Angie; Melanie; Rob; Dean; Maria; Claude; Bill; Tracy; Kevin; and myself. We were all current members of the chapter, however we did have a few non-members present for their first ghost-tracking experience: Joe*, Mary*, and Amy*.

The land that the cemetery now occupies has had a long past with settlers to the area. Once upon a time it was the home of the Piankeshaw Indians, a sub-tribe of the Miami Indian Nation, which chose to live separate from the rest of the ethnic group. However, the tribe's population dwindled, leaving the chief of the Piankeshaw to sign over the land to American settlers in 1818.

At first the land attracted many new settlers. However, as time passed, families moved out of the area, leaving their cemetery behind. Evidence of the many residents who have lived on the land through the centuries can still be found with a little digging: artifacts, such as arrow heads, nails, and even a ceremonial flagstone, have been found on the property around Cemetery X. Even the headstones within the cemetery tell the tale of those who once lived in the community there, with Civil War veterans and soldiers buried among their pioneering family members.

A Member's Experiences

Bill, an IGT member and a resident of the area, painstakingly organized the hunt the night of April 25, 2009. Thankfully the fickle Indiana weather held out for us that day, creating a good night to sit in a graveyard. Since it hadn't rained for a couple of days, the ground was still moist enough not to kick up dust in any photos we took; however, the cicadas were out in full force that night. As the group gathered, Bill started telling us why the chapter was in the cemetery that evening — he had his own personal experiences in the area that were so great that he thought they deserved investigation.

His first experience was when he was sixteen-years-old when, with a few buddies, he decided to explore around the old cemetery. According to his account, some of his friends trotted up ahead of the rest of the group...only to come shooting out of the cemetery a minute later. According to Bill's friends, when they approached the headstones of the cemetery, they could see two distinct balls of light dancing around the headstones; one red, the other green.

Another time one of his friends was parked in the cemetery waiting to scare up some trouble with some trespassers. While waiting in his truck, the man heard a knock from the back followed by a knock at the front of his cab. This puzzled that man since he knew no one was around. Suddenly, the temperature inside the truck's cab dropped sharply, which caused the man to become uneasy. Feeling as if something wanted him to leave, the man hauled it out of the cemetery to a more pleasant location.

IGT Bloomington members Dean and Maria listen to fellow chapter member Bill talk about his experiences in Cemetery X.

A week before the hunt, Bill and Melanie had visited the cemetery to assess its layout during the day, a common practice when setting up a hunt for many paranormal investigators. Bill took a camera along, snapping photos as they looked around the lonely cemetery. While walking along the eastern border, Bill turned to look over at the west side of the cemetery — and saw a Civil War soldier standing alone in the grass watching them along the graves! Quickly, Bill snapped a picture of the solider, which later revealed a shadowy apparition. The pair also encountered a warm guest of wind followed by a drastic temperature drop, as well as the foul smell of human urine or ammonia, while walking along the headstones. None of the phenomenon that they encountered could be explained, and thus the chapter decided to investigate the cemetery. Another odd thing Bill noted was that the pair heard a blood-curling scream after the wind touched their faces. However, he suspected that was a she-fox crying, and the timing was just a coincidence.

There have been other reports of paranormal events at Cemetery X. Travelers along the lonely and winding rural road have reported seeing "shadow people" darting along the headstones and the form of a person standing at the edge of the forest and then dissolving into thin air. Bill has also seen an apparition "distorting" the colors and background around it, along with a "pulsating" gravestone in one of the corners of the cemetery. The accounts of the strange and paranormal were myriad and incredible...but could they be true?

It didn't take long before members of the group started to experience odd occurrences on the cemetery grounds. We started our hunt at 9 p.m. — and by 9:10 Melanie had the first encounter of the night. Since our group was fairly large, we had fanned out into two groups of seven; one taking the east side and other the west side of the cemetery. Lisa and I were lagging behind the group looking over the west side when Melanie walked up to us. She didn't seem startled or upset, but she didn't hesitate to tell us that she had just seen something strange.

> "As I was walking over there [to where the cars were parked], something sounded like it was right behind me...footsteps. Then it stopped. I checked my flaps [of her bag], they weren't doing it. Then I saw what looked like a humanoid figure reflected in the car windows. I tried to reproduce it, but it was gone."

Rob, her husband, had also been walking with her when the strange incident took place, and described that the pair had felt the same warm gust of wind like when Melanie had visited a week prior, but this time it was followed by a severe cold spot.

We were standing around wondering what on earth Rob and Melanie had just experienced when one of the group members, Angie, reported that her camera batteries had died. Some paranormal investigators believe that when a spirit is trying to manifest, it will suck up all the energy available in the area. This can result in cold spots, but also makes victims out of batteries. When beginning a hunt or investigation, group members always make sure that they have fresh new batteries powering their equipment. The evening was not cold enough to have the temperature responsible for the power drain, so we were left wondering what had happened again. What was interesting to note is that Angie's camera turned on with the same set of batteries that had allegedly died as soon as we left the cemetery later that night.

Who's the Ghost?

After Melanie's report, Bill showed Lisa and I the headstones that had been rumored to "pulsate" light on occasion. The headstones in question are a group of limestone obelisks that are tucked away in one of the corners of the cemetery. The headstones all belong to the same family, but the headstone that is said to pulsate light the most is that of the father, who died in June of 1853.

Bill also showed the group the headstone of a young Civil War soldier who died at the young age of eighteen on February 10, 1862 at Fort Hughs. It is suspected that this soldier is the one who Bill saw standing in the cemetery since he is the only Civil War soldier buried there. The group performed an EVP session around the headstone during which Angie reported EMF spikes of .09 and .02, but the temperature remained consistent at 67.5 degrees. As we were asking questions, Tracy, who was holding one of the group's EMF detectors, reported that it had a complete battery drain. Almost as soon as she announced it, I heard footsteps and the sound of twigs breaking behind the large pine tree next to where our group was standing. I wasn't the only one who heard the footsteps either; Amy, who was standing beside me at the time, heard the sounds as well. Everyone was accounted for in the circle, and after investigating, no one could find what caused the sounds.

The EVP session ended at 9:30 with very little happening, so the group dispersed once again around the cemetery. Maria, Angie, Amy, and I moved around the pine tree to investigate what Amy and I had heard during the session a few minutes before. As we were looking at the foliage and twigs around the tree, Angie suddenly announced that she could smell something "like a really strong ammonia." Maria agreed and said the source of the smell was from a small limestone headstone that was engulfed with yucca plants. Could yucca plants produce such an odor? Never before had I ever smelled something so horrid...it smelled like a cat's litter box that hadn't been cleaned in ages. Bill and Lisa noticed that all four of us were plugging our noses and rushed over to

The Manann Headstone... IGT Bloomington member Melanie reads the engraved epitaph of the young soldiers.

see what the matter was. The smell disappeared from the area nearly as quickly as it showed up, so Bill and Lisa never detected it that night in the cemetery. We were left stumped as to what the cause of the smell was; animal markings that had been left there during the day? Was it the yucca plants secreting some type of odor? Whatever it was, it was unusual but not necessarily paranormal.

While the ladies in the group were caught up in the scent of urine seemingly out of nowhere, the guys in the group had their own equally mysterious experience while checking out a gravestone. Rob, Dean, and Joe were in the southeast corner of the cemetery taking pictures and reading names on the headstones. According to Rob, as they struggled to pronounce a particularly difficult family name on a headstone, they heard a woman's voice from behind them say it. At first they thought it was one of the female group members, but after looking around and realizing that they were the only ones in that part of the cemetery, they were left speechless. "I don't know if it was someone trying to explain the name or not," admitted Rob later.

We grouped up after strange experiences in the empty yard between where the cars were parked and the cemetery, roughly in the area where Bill had previously seen the apparition of the Civil War soldier to do a second formal EVP session. Melanie led the group while holding a K2 meter; Angie, who was standing to her right, was holding an EMF detector while Claude, across the circle, had a Gauss Meter. My own EMF detector lay just in front of me on the ground where I stood. The session started at 9:45 p.m. with little action, but all that changed two minutes into the recording.

What we experienced first was a strange silencing of the insects and forest noises during two particular questions at the beginning of the EVP session. Melanie asked if there were any children present with us in the cemetery and, in almost an acknowledgment of her question, the surrounding forest noises ceased for a full five seconds before returning to normal. A minute later Melanie asked, "Was that you standing in the corner behind the bush?" — a reference to a previous sighting of a black figure in the cemetery. Again all the forest noises went quiet for another five seconds. The phenomena never repeated itself again the rest of the time we stayed in the cemetery, and I honestly have no way of explaining how a forest full of insects and fauna could stop buzzing, hooting, or crying right when we asked questions.

Melanie then moved on to asking questions to the spirits present in the cemetery by communicating with the K2 Meter. It was instructed that any spirit who wanted to contact the group was to flash all five bulbs on the K2 for a "yes" once or flash all the bulbs multiple times in a row for a "no." At first nothing reacted to our questions, which in honesty is not an uncommon occurrence. Groups could be out all night at allegedly haunted sites and absolutely get nothing — no pictures, audio, or personal experiences of the paranormal kind. However, our watershed moment was when Melanie simply asked, "Can you tell us if anyone was here before?" The question was referencing previous visits she and Bill had made to the cemetery, and it tested whether or not a spirit kept its ability to remember intact, a sign of an intelligent haunt. Although there was no response to Melanie's question, Bill's follow up question did get one. He asked, "Can you name them?" BAM! There was a K2 hit of all five bulbs lighting up once for a "yes." That excited quite a few members, but one K2 hit does not make good data. Multiple hits however, do.

Bill quickly followed up with another question, "Do you recognize her [Melanie] being here before? If so, can you light it up?" There was a second K2 hit signaling "yes." Bill then asked if the spirit could light up the K2 meter the number of times Melanie had been to the cemetery and the meter lit up five distinct times in a row (which was dead on). Through the years, Melanie had visited the cemetery five times and this spirit remembered! Bill and Melanie kept generating questions and the spirit kept responding with accurate hits on the K2 meter; this went on for about three minutes. The group found out that the spirit was creating energy to talk to us, an interesting answer from the spirit world for an age-old question by paranormal investigators. Traditionally it is thought that spirits needed energy to manifest or communicate, as in the example of drained batteries. But this spirit was saying otherwise.

Melanie asked if it was okay if the group stayed in the cemetery for a while longer resulting with the KII meter vigorously lighting up to signal "no." It was at this time that I started to feel like our group was being watched by something behind me in the woods. The sensation felt like two piercing eyes heavily bearing down on me, the environment's pressure was so overwhelming that it made me feel very uneasy. I tried to dismiss the feeling as just my emotions running out of control, and asked Bill what kind of wildlife was known the roam in the area. We had seen a few deer in the woods and heard a few coyote calls, but Bill also told me that pumas have been sighted in the area as well. That gave me a very real thing to be concerned about, but the feeling of being watched didn't cease.

Just as suddenly as we had received responses from our K2 hits, they were gone. The group struggled to reconnect to the spirit or spirits in the cemetery, but was failing. In an attempt to connect, I asked, "Are you still here?" Half the circle was met with a much unexpected answer, an auditable "yes" from behind the group across the circle from me. I didn't hear it in real time; however, I did manage to record it on my digital voice recorder. Amy thought it sounded like a cat hissing while Joe thought the sound possibly came from a horse that was standing across the road from the cemetery. Melanie then felt a warm breeze like she did on a previous trip, but no one else in the group experienced it. She described the wind gust to be real warm followed by cold. Melanie asked Angie if she was catching any of the stuff going on with the other equipment and Angie replied, "It's all you."

This, though, wasn't the end of our night in Cemetery X. Near the end of our EVP session a very interesting turn of events happened. Bill exclaimed that as he was glancing towards Lisa and me, he had seen a shadow person walk directly behind me moving towards the cars. Maria had also caught sight of the same shadow person as Bill. Just as they were talking about what they had seen, I stepped back to readjust my stance. The funny thing was, I bumped into someone, and looking down I saw a gray boot under my shoe. All I could say was, "Bill, take a picture of my legs," which he immediately did. The photo revealed a gray mist swirling around my legs, just below my right knee. I originally thought that I had stepped on a mole hill, however after searching the ground where I was standing that proved to be incorrect.

We ended our night shortly after that encounter. It is customary for our group to close up a location with a prayer circle, a ritual to thank the spirits for communicating with us but requesting them to stay at that location. After we left many of the pieces of equipment that had malfunctioned in the cemetery started working again, leaving us to wonder what we had just experienced in that Cemetery.

Reflections

In all my years with IGT, I have visited very few locations that have proven to be active with unexplainable phenomena while we were investigating. I have been on more than twenty ghost hunts with the group and only two have proven to be completely and utterly bizarre...this was one of those locations. Cemetery X, in my opinion, is the most active place I have ever visited — perhaps one of the most active locations in the state for paranormal activity. From the people that I have spoken to about the cemetery, every time they visit they have had some odd experience; from being touched or seeing apparitions and shadow people. In the few hours we spent there, the group heard two different sets of disembodied voices, footsteps following us, and two different shadow people. Is this place haunted? Oh yes...very much so.

IU STUDENTS ENCOUNTER THE UNKNOWN

Residual Specter of University West

Nestled across from Read Residence Hall and east of the School of Music is a set of limestone apartment buildings known as the University Apartments. Completed in 1949 as post-war construction for the flood of returning GI students, these four-story limestone buildings offer 234 studio or one-bedroom apartments. For most of the twentieth century, these apartments were used for graduate or married student housing. However, with the ever-increasing wave of undergraduates to the university, they have been opened up to older undergraduate students. This is how I came to live in University Apartments West.

The Account

Traditionally, there are no ghost stories associated with either the East or West University apartment buildings. In the summer of 2005, fresh from my overseas exchange program in Japan, I moved into University Apartments to start a new school year. Helping me move in were my parents and my (then) fiancé, Mike. After dinner and a hard day's worth of work, we all retired to sleep. It was then I later learned from Mike that he had a very vivid dream about a young woman visiting the apartment. In his dream, he was hanging out in the apartment when he heard someone knocking on the front door. When he answered the door, he was greeted by a pretty blonde co-ed with long hair looking up at him. She was wearing jeans and white fitted t-shirt and asked if she could come in to visit. Although confused by her presence, he let her in. Mike woke up with a jolt, confused by the entire string of events in the dream.

Later that year I was working away at my computer desk on a paper for an anthropology class when, from the corner of my eye, I glimpsed a blond and white object moving across my room. Quickly looking to my left where the object was moving, I watched a figure of a young blond woman in a white t-shirt and jeans glide through my living room and into my bedroom. Curious, I jumped up and followed, only to lose her to the inky-darkness of my bedroom. Like many other ghost sightings before, she had no feet, but the rest of her details were visible albeit transparent. Perhaps most people would shake off the encounter as a side effect of working too long or staying up too late. Instead, I thought that was a pretty neat occurrence and continued with my work.

When Mike came to visit the following weekend, I remember telling him the story of seeing a female walk through the living room and into the bedroom. It was then he told me about his bizarre dream from a few months before. After sharing the details, we came to the conclusion that perhaps what we were seeing was the same imprinted memory. The building is made of limestone, like much of the campus, and a popular hypothesis states that limestone has the ability to hold energy longer than other building materials. Mike, a skeptic to ghost phenomena, just thought it was a coincidence, especially since no other phenomenon was reported to occur in the building or my apartment.

At first I agreed...until a year later. In nearly the same situation as the year prior I was working at my computer desk on yet another paper. I just happened to take a break to watch TV in the living room when right before my eyes she appeared again, wearing the same thing, walking the same way right into my bedroom. I followed again, losing her at the threshold of my bathroom door from my bedroom. She looked exactly the same, missing feet and all. It was then that I realized she really wasn't a ghost but rather a residual imprint of a former tenant. The woman could very well still be alive, just this imprinted event of her walking through the apartment remains to replay. Because of her general clothing, it is very hard to place what decade she is from, but because of her style of jeans, I tend to think the late 1980s to early 1990s since they were straight legged with a light wash with hints of bleach stains.

Reflections

I moved out of the apartment in 2007 when I graduated, moving onto bigger and brighter things. To this day I never have been able to identify who it could have been walking through the living room, and I now dearly wish that I had bothered to investigate into the situation further. I often wonder if the new tenants of that apartment have ever witnessed her, or if those who lived there before me ever have.

Mr. Squishy

Personal ghost stories or personal experiences aren't uncommon...most people at some point in their lives have had a brush with the unexplained. With roughly forty-eight percent of the population believing in ghosts, personal experiences with the paranormal can become a wild adventure into the unknown. Ashley's story is one of those wild accounts. Ashley is a friend and fellow Anthropology major from Indiana University Bloomington. It is her story coupled with the common Indiana University legends that gave me the idea to work on this book. We both have lived in Willkie Quadrangle in the past, albeit at different times.

A Bit of History

Compared to other dormitories, Willkie is quiet...*dead quiet*. Located between Rose Avenue and Union Street on the southeast corner of the campus, the double tower residence hall is named to honor IU alumnus Wendell L. Willkie. Born on February 18, 1892, in Elwood, Indiana, Willkie attended Indiana University Bloomington for a history degree. While there, he became a member of the Phi Theta Pi fraternity. After graduating, he had a brief stint as a history teacher before returning to IU to attend the School of Law. He graduated, served time in World War I as a first lieutenant in the U.S. Army, and eventually settled into Akron, Ohio, to work as a lawyer for the Firestone Rubber and Tire Company. There, he gained status in the local Democratic Party, eventually becoming a delegate to the 1924, 1929, and 1932 Democratic Conventions. In 1929, he moved his family to New York where he was hired as legal counsel for the electric holding company Commonwealth & Southern and rose through the ranks. Eventually he became its president in 1933.

Although he was a supporter of President Franklin Roosevelt in the 1932 election, Willkie became disillusioned when the new president proposed the Tennessee Valley Authority (TVA), a government-run program that supplied electricity to the poor and rural towns within the Tennessee Valley. The TVA would become direct competition to private electric companies supplying electricity to the area, Willkie's Commonwealth & Southern Co. being one such company. Although the TVA was good program in theory, the government-run program would create strong competition financially that other private and smaller companies could not compete with and eventually lead to a government held monopoly on electricity in the Tennessee Valley. Although Willkie testified against the TVA program to the House of Representatives in April 1933, his attempts to halt its creation failed. In 1939, Willkie had to sell the Commonwealth & Southern Company for $78.6 million since it could no longer financially compete with the government-run TVA program, as he had predicted.

This turn of events forced him to re-think his political party choices, so in 1939 he officially joined the Republican Party. He then started the road that made him a notable person in history by becoming the Republican nominee for President of the United States in the 1940 election. He lost to Franklin Roosevelt with Roosevelt's 27 million votes to Willkie's 22 million. In the Electoral College, it was 449 to 82. After the 1940 election, Willkie became an ally with some of President Roosevelt's political plans and was a very strong anti-racism activist. In 1941, he became a partner in the New York City law firm Miller, Boston, and Owen; making it Willkie, Owen, Otis, Farr, and Gallagher. That law firm is now known as Willkie, Farr, and Gallagher. He did make a bid for the 1944 presidential election, but was not as successful on the second try due to his progressive theology. Although Willkie survived several heart attacks, on October 8, 1944 he died of heart disease. He was only fifty-two years old.

In 1969, Willkie Quadrangle was completed, a two-tower dormitory initially reserved for students twenty-one or older, much like the Eigenmann Residence Center built five years prior. In 1999, however, the quadrangle went through a major renovation, making it one of the nicest residence centers on campus. Unlike the double-occupant rooms in many of the other dormitories, Willkie plays host to double room suites, with each room being a single occupant with a bathroom joining the two. Each room has their own temperature controls and university provided furniture of a bed, dresser, shelves, and computer desk.

Things that Go "Bump" in the Night

In fall 2005, Ashley moved in as an upperclassman into the North Tower. Just after moving into her new room, though, she began to notice that the florescent light bulb on her computer desk would dim and brighten randomly. At first she thought nothing about it.

"I only noticed that whenever the light flickered, I would feel so cold," recalled Ashley.

A loose connection in a florescent light bulb isn't an uncommon issue in dormitory life; however Ashley noticed that although she and her roommate's rooms were set at the same temperature, her room always felt several degrees colder.

"I had maintenance come and take a look at the light and the heating system, but they said nothing was wrong and I left it at that."

Ashley lived in the unexplainably chilly room for weeks before something strange started to happen — the closet door began to open on its own accord! All of the doors in Willkie Quadrangle are made from the same heavy wood. When I lived there I always found them quite the workout to open, especially when your hands are full of books or groceries. The pneumatics installed on the doors were also set high, so opening the closet door took a certain level of physical effort and the doors closed slowly afterwards.

Ashley, knowing my interest in the paranormal, consulted me on the issues she was having in her dorm room, but whenever I visited the room, I couldn't find anything amiss. Ashley attempted to explain why the door was opening on its own, but try as she may, she couldn't figure out how the door kept opening. It wasn't her roommate doing it because Ashley would lock the door that led into the bathroom, which linked their rooms.

 "For the next couple of days I made absolutely sure that there was nothing in the way of the closet door. Yet every morning, like a sunrise, that door would be open!"

Things took a wild turn in late February 2006 when Ashley *met* her spectral roommate. Still amazed by the experience, she recalls:

 "I was safe and snug in my bed [when] I was awakened, I would say about two in the morning, with a jolt by the certainty that someone was in bed with me!"

Ashley knew for a fact that the doors were locked and she did not have a boyfriend at the time.

 "I knew with every fiber of my being that the entity, ghost, whatever, was male and apparently liked to cuddle. Why a ghost would want to hop into bed with me is beyond me, but I knew what I felt!"

Ashley kept me up on the turn of unexplained events happening in her dorm room. When she told me that the ghost crept into her bed one night, she decided to codename him "Mr. Squishy," so we were able to keep talking about him in the presence of others in public while not letting on that it had to do with the paranormal. Why the name Mr. Squishy? It just sounded good at the time. Mr. Squishy returned to visit Ashley nearly once a week after the initial visit. He would sometimes cuddle up to Ashley in her twin bed in the middle of the night or sometimes showing up as wisps of fog or mist in her room. Mr. Squishy's signature move was to always open the closet door and flicker the desk light as he entered the room.

The school year ended and Ashley moved out, never learning the identity of her nightly 'visitor'. She says that by the end of her stay in Willkie, "I was kinda of blasé about the whole thing," noting that while her experience was bizarre, it was never scary. However, Ashley was quick to add that she wasn't "keen on experiencing [this] again."

The Real Mr. Squishy?

Mr. Squishy tends to be one of the sweetest, albeit creepiest ghost experiences I have ever run across. He just seemed to be a bit lonely and appeared to favor Ashley and her spunky nature over the other students residing in her building at the time. While looking into the history of Willkie, I did come across an article from April 1990 that appeared in Bloomington's *Herald*

Times, the city's local newspaper. According to the article, an eighteen-year-old freshman named Michael who lived in Willkie Quadrangle's south tower was found hanging in his dorm room closet. His death was ruled either an accident or suicide by the local coroner. To this date, there have been no other deaths associated with Willkie Quadrangle.

Reflections

Was it the spirit of Michael visiting Ashley on a weekly basis in her dorm room in 2006, sixteen years after his death? We may never know for sure, however this case is an interesting one, being a good example of the living and the dead relating to each other without the pre-conceived notions of fear pulling down the entire relationship. Although Ashley isn't keen on repeating the experience later in life, she did not mind living with a ghost while she was there. In a way, it seems the two learned from one another: Ashley learning that perhaps our spirit continues on after death and Mr. Squishy learning that interaction with others isn't a negative experience. There is something else to note: Michael was found dead in the south tower of Willkie, but Ashley lived in the north tower. Is it possible for ghosts to actually freely move about the location where they died, even if they aren't physically linked? I also wonder what new people Mr. Squishy is meeting now in Willkie Quadrangle....

Sara's Story

Located along the tree lined East Third Street right off the campus is a string of impressive sorority houses. Currently there are twenty-three sororities active on Indiana University Bloomington's campus, most of which have their own sorority house. This following story is about once such sorority at the University, which I refer to as Alpha Omega to protect its identity.

The Account

Initially, when I started researching for this book, I didn't know any stories about ghosts or paranormal phenomena coming out of the sororities or fraternities at Indiana University. Since then I have stood corrected, finding many accounts of paranormal activity surrounding the Greek life on campus.

Meeting Sara was a chance encounter; we were not acquainted while attending the university, but had become friends after graduation when we were introduced to each other as IU alumni. In a city full of Ohio State University folk, meeting a fellow Hoosier is a wonderful thing and it wasn't long before Sara confided that her former sorority house just off IU's campus on Third Street had a ghost.

"I can't remember if it was a founder or somebody who lived there," she said, but whenever something odd happened around the house the sorority sisters would blame the "Alpha Omega ghost." Things like the air-conditioning unit making hissing and popping sounds, the random disappearance of small objects such as cell phone chargers or keys, and frequent plumbing issues were all attributed to the invisible resident of the century-old house.

One year during her stay in the house, Sara moved into a small second floor room located next to a dysfunctional bathroom. "When I moved to the second floor, we had all kinds of plumbing issues and really weird things happened in my room because it was next to the bathroom," said Sara.

The toilet would constantly flush and odd banging and clanging was heard. Plumber after plumber would leave scratching their heads, at a loss as to what was happing and how to fix it. Although the bathroom was repaired and remodeled several times, the issues kept returning.

One night Sara and her roommate were hanging out in their room as their Alpha Omega sisters came in to check their names off a list and retrieve a screen-printed t-shirt for an upcoming Greek Life event. Sara's roommate was the coordinator for the t-shirts used at this event and, during this time, kept an order list of all the shirts made. This list sat on top of a coffee stable beside the television that Sara was watching. Keeping an eye on the list so it wouldn't get lost, Sara would occasionally chat with visitors to the room as they collected their shirts. It was when Sara looked away for a second to greet a visitor that catastrophe happened — out of nowhere the order list had somehow become drenched in water!

"The table was in the middle of the room, nothing near it, and it got soaking wet! Soaking wet! Like, absolutely drenched, all the ink was gone! You couldn't figure out what was on it," explained Sara.

The duo went to work searching for the cause in the room, but the pipes were dry and nothing was leaking from the ceiling. Sara noted that neither of the girls or their visitors had any beverages in the room, so it was a complete mystery how the order list could have become wet. The girls blamed the odd incident on the Alpha Omega ghost.

This incident did not just occur once however; it repeated itself a few months later when the girls were working on distributing t-shirts for another upcoming event for the sorority. In the same scenario as before, the order list sat on the center of the table in the room. Again, when Sara turned away for a second to talk to a fellow sorority sister, she returned to a soaking wet mess on the table. The girls, remembering the earlier situation, looked all over the room for the source of the water, but failed to find it.

Drenching of order lists wasn't the end of the girls' unexplainable experiences while living in the sorority house. On several occasions their room door would open and close on its own. At first they thought it was a fellow sister playing a prank on them, but after investigating, they couldn't find a culprit. "We had weird energy in that room," reflected Sara. "We thought it was caused by a draft since the house was old, but it always opened and closed on its own." This occurrence only helped to increase the creepy vibes that the girls felt in their bedroom....

Reflections

To this day no one has been able to explain what occurred those months Sara lived in that room. Although it was eerie at times, Sara never worried about her wellbeing there. She never felt that the eerie presence in the house was malevolent, but it did make the hairs on her arm stand up a few times. Perhaps it is a stroke of bad luck with the plumbing that caused it all, or perhaps it is the Alpha Omega ghost attempting to entertain the fraternity girls through small pranks and paranormal mischief. It was suggested one time that perhaps nearby spirits were attracted to Sara's room because the water was acting as a conducting agent. In a more mystical light, it could be that Sara's sorority room was involved with a spiritual vortex of some kind, but like many things in the great wide world around us, we may never know.

The Banta Spirit

Not all who live on Indiana University Bloomington's campus are undergraduate students. Like many universities its size, IUB has a hardy flock of older students in its masters and doctorate programs. For the families of such students, living in the married student housing in the northeast residence neighborhood is an option. Located within walking distance to the Kelley School of Business, psychology building, and other college buildings, the cluster of married student apartments known as BBHN is a convenient choice.

Brief Background

The apartments known as Banta, Bicknell, Hepburn, and Nutt were originally built in 1955 to house the growing number of post-war married students. Four years later, the four apartment buildings were given their current names. Most of the student body simply knows them as BBHN, an abbreviation of all four of the married student buildings names. The community is comprised of four limestone-frame buildings that contain a total of 141 one- and two-bedroom apartments only for married students. Banta and Nutt are comprised of two-story townhouses, each containing two bedroom apartments which come unfurnished. The neighborhood, like many of the dormitories around campus, is a mix of domestic and international students plus their families.

Experiences

Unlike the other residence buildings on campus, few ghost stories have come out of this neighborhood, but that does not necessarily mean there is an absence of strange occurrences of the unknown taking place there. For Melanie and Rob Hunter, they had an intriguing experience living with a ghost in their apartment in the Banta building.

From 1989 until 1992, Melanie lived on campus with Rob and her two sons. The first paranormal encounter occurred one evening when the pair were alone in the apartment.

"I heard something one night, we had heard it in Rob's apartment a year or two before," started Melanie. "We were lying on the bed, and it was very hot, so we were lying on the bed with our heads at the foot of the bed trying to catch some extra breeze."

After Rob had fallen asleep, Melanie heard someone whisper, "Rob," beside the bed. Immediately, she woke Rob up asking if he had heard the voice, which, of course, he hadn't. This wasn't the first time a disembodied voice had called out to Rob...the exact same thing happened years earlier in Rob's old apartment.

Odd occurrences picked up after that, including objects jumping off the walls onto the floor. Melanie would also find her keys moved from place to place around the apartment seemingly on their own. "I would lay my keys down nowhere near the edge [of a table] or anything. And I would come back and they would be on the floor," she said, calmly recounting her experiences.

Rob and one of the sons would also hear footsteps above them in the apartment from time to time. He remembers going upstairs in Banta one night. Dropping his voice down to a whisper, he said, "I heard someone say 'someone's coming.'"

For some, electronics acting out of character sometimes has been associated with the supernatural. Rob and Melanie had issues with their television's VCR for a period of time while living in the apartment. According to Melanie, the VCR would keep flipping back and forth between rewinding and winding tapes inside the unit. Upon reflecting on the incident, Melanie said, "I guess there could have been something wrong, but it has never done that." Nor has that unit acted out of hand since.

The strangest event to occur at the apartment happened one night while Melanie's sons were away. Although the family had never felt intimidated or threatened while living in the apartment, one bizarre event caused Melanie to be worried about their situation. Melanie said it started when, for one reason or another, she needed to enter the boys' bedroom.

"As soon as I walked through the door, I felt this very uneasy, threatening, thing," she recalled.

What came next was even more startling. Standing in the room and sensing the change in atmosphere, she heard this strange deep raspy voice say 'Boys.' "It scared me, [and] I backed out of there," said Melanie, who didn't return to that room for the rest of the evening.

Eventually Melanie and Rob moved out of their Banta apartment into a larger home in Bloomington. The couple suspect, however, that whatever had been residing in the apartment has somehow followed them to their new home. Their anxiety was quelled with the addition to the family — a dog. Apparently whatever had followed the couple around didn't take to dogs too well.

Melanie and Rob's experiences while residing in the Banta apartments eventually led them to join IGT Bloomington through a friend in 2007. Since then, the pair have been to numerous haunted locations and have seen plenty of other unexplained phenomena. It remains a question just what it was that seemed to be living among Melanie and Rob in their old apartment. It cannot be said for certain if it was a poltergeist or some other form of paranormal activity, or even perhaps a mix of both.

Phantom Legs on Third Street

I saw many strange and awesome things while attending IU's main campus in Bloomington. Cardboard boat regattas, tie-dyed snowmen, a gargoyle that looks like Donald Duck standing proud wearing a mortarboard, vest, and glasses on top of Goodbody Hall, and a pair of walking legs on Third Street — yes, you didn't misread...a walking pair of legs on Third Street.

Admittedly, I have seen my share of ghostly apparitions through my short lifetime on this earth. It all started when I witnessed the full-bodied apparition of my grandfather walk up the staircase in my parents' house at two in the morning at the age of nine. Since then, I have witnessed shadow people, orbs, and a purple floating head in my rear-view mirror. Seeing these odd specters is one reason why I became a paranormal investigator in the first place! They are all wonderful personal encounters to retell, but the pair of legs was probably the oddest phantom I have ever encountered.

Stories about ghostly limbs haunting locations are not new; many of the accounts from England, Japan, and other places in America

This was one of the strangest ghost encounters I've ever had. *Illustration by Kat Klockow.*

recount ghostly arms, hands, or even heads haunting specific buildings, bridges, and roads. Hey, if there are headless horsemen and other apparitions roving around this world, it only makes sense that the disembodied limbs could also do so! Usually, the sight of just a floating body part traumatizes the witnesses so badly that they refuse to return to the location where they had seen it!

It was the late spring of 2006, nearing finals time for the students at IU when this episode happened. I was wrapping up my fourth year attending the university, feverishly working on anthropology papers and translating chapters of books from Japanese to English for courses I was taking. I have always been a night owl, often staying up until two or three in the morning. On this particular night, I decided that my brain had enough looking through pages of Japanese text and dearly needed a break, so I made my way out the apartment building to the intersection of Third Street and Jordan

Avenue. At the time I lived in University Apartments West, and a convenience store sat diagonally across from the apartment building. It had become a sort of ritual for me to take a break around midnight to walk across to the store, pick up a snack, and return to studying. As I stood waiting for the light to change so I could cross, I noticed a pair of legs walking east on the other side of the street. The leggy apparition appeared on the sidewalk in front of Bear's Place, a local eatery, and traveled east down Third Street, crossed Jordan Avenue, and faded as it approached the Golden Dragon Chinese Restaurant. The legs were wearing a pair of tight fit, faded blue jeans with slip on shoes, much like the brand Vans produces. A shiny white belt could barely be made out as the apparition faded above what would be the navel. At the time no other pedestrians were around, I was alone to watch the ghost make its way across the street. All I could do was chuckle to myself about the spirit I had just witnessed; I had seen too many more terrifying ones to be scared of a pair of legs.

Reflections

Looking back, the ghost only manifested for a brief period of time, about five seconds, just long enough to cross the street. In fact, many tragic road accidents have happened around that area of campus. With the School of Music located at the northwest corner of Third and Jordan, the intersection being a crossroads for throngs of students living in the Northeast neighborhood of campus, as well as Third Street being a major thoroughfare for drivers between the east and west sides of Bloomington along the campus, accidents happen. Students have been hit while crossing the street, cars have run into each other in the intersection, and tragically some students have been killed by drunken drivers while walking along the sidewalks. Interestingly enough, this is the area where the Lady in Black has also been seen walking along the road.

Perhaps what I saw was the ghost of a one-time student of the university? It was suggested to me upon the retelling of my experience by a fellow ghost hunter that perhaps the spirit in life had self confidence issues, and thus only appeared as a pair of legs. This is all speculation of course, but that hypothesis holds water given the age group of the student body. So maybe if you are traveling along Third Street in the wee hours of the morning in late spring, you too will happen upon the phantom legs of Third Street. And if you are really lucky, maybe run into the Lady in Black as well!

BIBLIOGRAPHY

"About the Folklore Institute." Accessed March 18, 2009, at www.indiana.edu/~folklore/folk_history.html.

"Alpha Hall." Accessed March 23, 2009, at www.bloomingpedia.org/wiki/alpha_hall.

Baker, Ronald L. *Hoosier Folk Legends*. Bloomington, Indiana: Indiana University Press, 1982.

"Ballantine Hall." Accessed March 23, 2009, at www.bloomingpedia.org/wiki/ballantine_hall.

Blair, Brian. "Storied Crump's future uncertain." *The Republic*, February 24, 2008.

"Blasts from the Past: 50 years of alumni folklore." *Traditions: Alumni Newsletter*. Indiana University, fall 2003.

Boyd, James. "IU student survives apparent suicide attempt." *Herald Times*, April 19, 2004.

    "Man fall from IU building: student survives drop from eighth floor of Ballantine Hall in apparent suicide try." *Herald Times*, April 20, 2004.

    "IU student still in hospital after drop." *Herald Times*, April 21, 2004.

Brodsy, Alyson. "Ballantine's near 50-year history marked by suicide, sex." *The Indiana Daily Student*, January 19, 2006.

Brook, R. "Azailia's Headless Ghost Gal." Indiana Ghost Trackers Ghost Stories, March 19, 2009 (www.indianaghosts.org).

Brunvand, Jan Harold. *Encyclopedia of Urban Legends*. New York, New York: W.W. Norton & Company, 2001.

"Coroner rules death suicide." *Herald Times*, November 23, 2000.

"County Coroner can't say whether hanging was accident or suicide." *Herald Times*, April 16, 1990.

Cutter, Chip. "Folklore ghost walk takes student past IU spooks." *The Indiana Daily Student*, October 27, 2005.

Ebling, Jennifer. "Haunted Indiana University and the Ghosts of Bloomington." *Associated Content*, May 23, 2008 (www.associatedcontent.com/article/760475/haunted_indiana_university_and_the.html).

    "Ghosts and Legends of Indiana's Stepp Cemetery." Associated Content, October 19, 2007. (www.associatedcontent.com/article/417148/ghosts_and_legends_of_indianas_stepp.html).

"Eigenmann Hall." Accessed March 22, 2009, at www.bloomingpedia.org/wiki/Eigenmann_Hall.

"Elisha Ballantine." Accessed March 23, 2009, at www.bloomingpedia.org/wiki/elisha_ballantine.

Faine, Jackie. "Folklore of Student Life: 11th Floor Fear." Fall 1996, Indiana University.

    "Folklore of Student Life: A hot topic in the Stacks." Fall 2005, Indiana University.

    "Folklore of Student Life: Just beyond the elevator." Fall 2005, Indiana University.

    "Folklore of Student Life: No sturdy ground." Fall 2005, Indiana University.

    (All articles accessed March 10, 2009 at www.indiana.edu/~f351jmcd/legends.html.)

Ghostly Talk. "Ghostly Talk Crew's Experiences at Whispers Estate." December 30, 2007.

    "Doug's Trip to Whispers Estate." November 4, 2007.

Glasgow, Rebecca. "Campus ghost walks reveal secrects of local haunts." *The Indiana Daily Student*, October 25, 2006.

Hall, Dan T. "Ghost Stories II: Unmasking the Dead." Vizmo Films, 2008.

Halpern, Maura. "'Tales' from campus: 'Ghost Walk' tells campus ghost stories tales of legends." *The Indiana Daily Student*, October 31, 2002.

Hammans, Justin, and John Michael Talboo. "Stepp Cemetery." *The Encyclopedia of Haunted Places*. Ed. Jeff Belanger. Edison, New Jersey: Castle Books, 2005.

Hancuff, John. "Eerie stories draw curiousity seekers, vandals to Stepp Cemetery" and "My night in the Stepp Cemetery." *Herald Times*, August 12, 2001.

    "Update: Another Stepp Cemetery myth bites the dust." *Herald Times*, August 26, 2001.

Hart, Brittney. "Crump: Ghost topic of spirited discussion." *The Republic*, April 14, 2007.

Higgs, Steven. "Murder at IU: Crime was the first of its kind on campus." *Herald Times*, April 26, 1992.

    "New coroner's inquest sought in 1960 'suicide'." *Herald Times*, December 20, 1988.

    "Time runs out in 1960 death case." *Herald Times*, April 16, 1990.

Hofstetter, Rick. "Is Story Haunted?" and "History of Story, Indiana." Accessed July 15, 2009, at www.storyinn.com.

"Home Spotlight: Mitchell house straight out of 'the Twilight Zone.'" *Herald Times*, May 21, 2005.

Hoosier Paranormal Research. "Case #10: The Story Inn" and "Case #12: The Crump Theater." Accessed July 20, 2009, at www.hoosierparanormal.com.

Horn, David. "Ghost trackers roam halls of IMU." *Herald Times*, April 13, 2003.

Hoyer, Meghan. "Campus lore explains almost everything: These stories about IU might not all be true, but folk tales about ghosts and traditions are fun to tell." *Herald Times*, September 7, 1996.

Hunter, Rob. "Indiana Ghost Trackers report of paranormal investigation: Raintree House." Indiana Ghost Trackers Bloomington, May 31, 2008.

Hyde, Laura Jane. "Ghost Hunting: Local group searches for evidence of paranormal activity." *Indiana Daily Student*, October 30, 2005.

Incollingo, Larry. "A Tunnel of Tales." *Herald Times*, November 29, 1992.

    "Self-appointed caretaker devoted to campus cemetery." *Herald Times*, September 17, 1989.

"Indiana University." Accessed March 10, 2009, at www.hauntedhouses.com/states/in/indiana_university.cfm.

Janosch, Brian. "Ain't afraid of no ghosts: Campus ghost trackers discover haunted folklore in University buildings." *The Indiana Daily Student*, November 18, 2003.

John, Tracy. "Folklore of Student Life: The Chapel." Indiana University. Accessed March 10, 2009, at www.indiana.edu/~f351jmcd/legends.html.

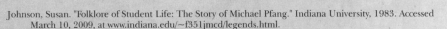

Johnson, Susan. "Folklore of Student Life: The Story of Michael Pfang." Indiana University, 1983. Accessed March 10, 2009, at www.indiana.edu/~f351jmcd/legends.html.

Kearns, Colin. "'Death' comes to IU at annual campus ghost walk: Halloween event features historic tales of spooks, murder." *The Indiana Daily Student*, October 27, 2003.

Klassen, Teri. "Gravestones at Dunn Cemetery mark family's history." *Herald Times*, March 18, 1992.

Lattanner, Leah. "Folklore of Student Life: Campus Legends." Indiana University, fall 2005.

"Folklore of Student Life: Dorm Legends." Indiana University, fall 2005.

"Folklore of Student Life: Ghost Legends." Indiana University, fall 2005.

"Folklore of Student Life: Legends." Indiana University, fall 2005.

(All articles accessed March 10, 2009, at www.indiana.edu/~f351jmcd/legends.html.)

Leonard, Mike. "The Puzzle of Porticos' Haunting." *Herald Times*, November 8, 1988.

"Showers Family holds Bloomington Homecoming." *Herald Times*, September 24, 1989.

Lewis, Mike. "Reasonable Skeptics." *Times Mail*, August 3, 2007.

"Man plunges to death at Ballantine." *Herald Times*, August 20, 1999.

Marimen, Mark. *Haunted Indiana*. Grand Rapids, Michigan: Thunder Bay Press, 1997.

Marimen, Mark, James A. Willis, and Troy Taylor. *Weird Indiana*. New York, New York: Sterling, 2008.

Matson, Donald. "Rose Hill Cemetery." Accessed March 18, 2009, at www.bloomington.gov.

Mccawley, Harry. "Just as many suspected: Crump Theater has ghosts." *The Republic*, April 4, 2006.

McIlveen, Rose, and Ellen Mathia. "Basements, Tunnels, Nooks, and Crannies." Home Pages Indiana University, October 18, 1996 (www.iuinfo.indiana.edu/homepages/1018/1018text/under.html).

McPhearson, Colleen. "Folklore of Student Life: The Gazebo" and "Folklore of Student Life: The Showalter Fountain." Indiana University, fall 1983. Accessed March 10, 2009, at www.indiana.edu/~f351jmcd/legends.html.

Mikkelson, Barbara. "Arm and Stammer." Accessed June 17, 2009, at www.snopes.com/horrors/gruesome/cadaver.asp.

Mitchell, Whitney. "IU's Underground." *The Indiana Daily Student*, March 28, 2007.

"Morgan-Monroe State Forest." Accessed April 7, 2009, at www.en.wikipedia.org/wiki/morgan-monroe_state_forest.

Murphy, Katy. "Creepy campus tales set Halloween mood: Folklorists' IU legends keep audience spooked." *Herald Times*, October 31, 2002.

Nissen, Sam. "Scared to death: IU home to gaggle of ghastly hauntings." *The Indiana Daily Student*, July 18, 2005.

Norman, Michael, and Beth Scott. *Haunted America*. New York, New York: Tor Books, 1994.

Nosko, David. "Annual ghost walk explores spooky legends, myths around campus: Graduate students dress up, play roles of haunted figures." *The Indiana Daily Student*, October 22, 2004.

Renier, Van. "What keeps ghost hunters coming back, time and again" and "Whispers Estate History." Accessed June 2, 2009, at www.whispersestate.net.

Rodriguez, Mercedes. "Places of the past provide connection to IU's history." *Herald Times*, October 20, 2005.

Sechrest, David. "The Crump Theater." Accessed August 10, 2009, at http://www.historiccolumbusindiana.com.

Semig, Doug. "About Whispers Estate: Just Say No to Orbs Tour." Waverly, New York: Waverly Opera House, March 14-16, 2008.

Shawgo, Kaitlin. "Ghoul School: IU is rich with ghost stories, legends." *Indiana Daily Student*, October 31, 2007.

Sheckler, Jackie. "New Owner Adds Chapter to Story Inn." *Herald Times*, January 27, 1999.

Silas, Alexis, and Alyson Brodsy. "Spirits abound on Campus: University setting provides ample haunting ground for ghosts and ghouls." *Indiana Daily Student*, October 31, 2000.

Slaten, Krystal. "Beyond the Grave: In 'haunted' Mitchell home, walls really do talk," "Favorite Haunt: Mitchell home is source of spooky stories," and "Haunted house's history." *Times Mail*. August 2, 2007.

"Everybody's Talk'n: Ghost's Abound" and "Everybody's Talk'n: Wanted: Exorcist." *Times Mail*, August 10, 2007.

Smith, Julie. "Folklore of Student Life: Got that sinking feeling." Indiana University, 1996. Accessed March 10, 2009, at www.indiana.edu/~f351jmcd/legends.html.

Thay, Edrick. *Ghost Stories of Indiana*. Edmonton, Canada: Ghost House Books, 2001.

Thorkelson, Berit. "A Room with a Boo." *Midwest Living*, October 2004.

Tucker, Elizabeth. *Campus Legends: A Handbook*. Westport, Connecticut: Greenwood Press, 2005.

Haunted Halls: Ghostlore of American College Campuses. Jackson, Mississippi: University Press of Mississippi, 2007.

Welsh-Huggins, Andrew. "IU shooting victims dies from injuries." *Herald Times*, April 29, 1992.

Werner, Nick. "Students work to restore landmark." *The Republic*, January 30, 2004.

Werth, Brian. "Porticos Restaurant closing for good." *Herald Times*, June 23, 1992.

Willis, Wanda Lou. *Haunted Hoosier Trails: A Guide to Indiana's Famous Folklore Spooky Sites*. Zionsville, Indiana: Guild Press Emmis Publishing, LP., 2002.

More Haunted Hoosier Trails. Cincinnati, Ohio: Clerisy Press, 2004.

Wilson, Doug. "Story Celebrates 150 years: Revitalized Brown County village marks occasion with concert Saturday." *Herald Times*, August 9, 2009.

Withered, Elise. "Folklore of Student Life: Stepp Cemetery." Indiana University, 1983. Accessed March 10, 2009, at http://www.indiana.edu/~f351jmcd/legends.html.

Young, Marian. "CFC finds buyer for Porticos Property: Developer Dvorak plans 'more conservative' project on site of rejected high rise." *Herald Times*, February 13, 1995.

INDEX